A VOICE FOR WILDLIFE

ALSO BY VICTOR B. SCHEFFER

The Year of the Whale

The Year of the Seal

The Seeing Eye

with decorations by UGO MOCHI

CHARLES SCRIBNER'S SONS · NEW YORK

A VOICE FOR WILDLIFE

by Victor B. Scheffer

The poem "The Harpooning" from *The Night Bathers* by Ted Walker
is used with the permission of Jonathan Cape
Ltd. © 1969 The New Yorker Magazine, Inc.

Library of Congress Cataloging in Publication Data

Scheffer, Victor B.
  A voice for wildlife.

  Includes bibliographical references.
  1.Wildlife conservation.   2. Wildlife management.
I.   Title.
QL82.S33   639   73-19290
ISBN 0-684-13714-3

1 3 5 7 9 11 13 15 17 19 V/C 20 18 16 14 12 10 8 6 4 2

Printed in the United States of America

The time will come, when humanity will extend its mantle over every thing which breathes. We have begun by attending to the condition of slaves; we shall finish by softening that of all the animals which assist our labours or supply our wants.

—Jeremy Bentham, Principles of Penal Law

❧ CONTENTS

ix

Contents

A VOICE FOR WILDLIFE

Introduction

My father, Theophilus Scheffer, who died in his hundredth year, once told me that he could not be blamed for exterminating the passenger pigeon, because the only time he had a shot at one, he missed. The last pigeon died in the Cincinnati Zoo when I was eight years old. Now that I am retired from duty as a biologist in the federal government, I have had long hours to think about my father, and about the silver-gray pigeon, and about all lost, wild America. Father was born in 1867. He saw the beginnings of the Age of Petroleum, the Age of Electricity, and the Age of Nuclear Power. I am alive at the beginning of the Age of Ecology, or, if you wish, the Age of Environmental Awareness, or the Age of the New Conservation.

These beginnings are historic points of acceleration marking the onset of qualitative as well as quantitative changes. In the century from 1870 to 1970, the population of the United States rose from 40 million to 204 million and the gross national product rose from $9 billion to $1,000 billion, but such numbers do not reflect the truly important changes, which are in human attitudes, moral values, and priorities. Father would have called these changes in the spiritual condition of man.

Because I have lived through a period of remarkable change and because I am a naturalist, I have set myself the task of tracing the evolution of a new wildlife ethic in North America. The evolution is in fact a quiet revolution. The way men will "use" wildlife in the future will be sharply unlike that in the past. Today hunters are engaged in an ideological war with nonhunters, and trappers with nontrappers. These and similar areas of controversy call for examination.

This revolution, like many others, began in the ranks of youth, in that wondrous company where one can afford the luxury of ideals and can easily fall in love with the image of what man could be. Though young people in all times have been skeptical and rebellious, prone to see failure and hypocrisy in the lives of their elders more clearly than accomplishment and truth, the generation gap which began to open in the 1960s has now become remarkably wide. The young people of today are advancing through analytical or conceptual intelligence to what the English philosopher Patrick Corbett has called "the kinds of intuitive or imaginative intelligence displayed by cats, mothers and poets." [1]

I was gently amused, a year ago, when my students

in zoology at the University of Washington objected to using ordinary mouse traps to catch small animals for study. So, instead, we set out a string of live-traps and after watching our captives for a while released them to scurry away through the sagebrush. A small affair, but thought-provoking.

Yet the new look at wildlife conservation is not the insight of youth alone. Every generation has had adults who held the clear, uncluttered vision of youth. Henry David Thoreau, John Burroughs, John Muir, George Bird Grinnell, Theodore Roosevelt, Liberty Hyde Bailey, Aldo Leopold, Olaus Johan Murie, and Rachel Carson are growing in prophetic stature because the words they spoke in their time are increasingly recognized as truth.

Prophets must of course be judged in the context of their time. Beyond the faces of Grinnell and Roosevelt we see dimly the mounted heads of trophy birds and beasts. Though champions of wildlife, those hunting men could never quite see animals except as pieces in some enormous game. The Boone and Crockett Club, a strong organization today with headquarters in the Carnegie Museum, Pittsburgh, was founded by Roosevelt in 1887; its letterhead still reads: "For Sport with the Rifle and Conservation." We can sympathize more readily with the purpose of the club if we remember that it came into being in a conservation vacuum.

The revolution in wildlife conservation was given respectability in 1972 by a world conference, the full impact of which is yet to be measured. On June 5 to 16,

1972, the United Nations Conference on the Human Environment met at Stockholm, attended by delegates of 114 nations, by accredited observers of about 500 organizations, and by unofficial representatives of about 500 other organizations. Never before had such numbers assembled to consider the task of earthkeeping. The representatives of the newly developing nations were not quite sure that they could afford wildlife at the (supposed) expense of economic improvement; those of the older nations were convinced that healthy wildlife populations are an indication of a country in which people are living in balance with natural resources. On the last day, the conference accepted a Declaration on the Human Environment which read, in part:

"Man has a special responsibility to safeguard and wisely manage the heritage of wildlife and its habitat which are now gravely imperiled by a combination of adverse factors. Nature conservation including wildlife must therefore receive importance in planning for economic development."

Despite ideological, political, economic, and religious differences, the men and women at Stockholm were able to agree that "the Earth is a closed ecological system and man continues to modify it only at his peril." [2]

❧

THE ideological revolution can be explained as a new awareness, first, that wildlife populations and their homelands all over the world are going down the drain, and, second, that killing, whether it be of people in political wars and in electric chairs or of animals in the wild, can be erosive to the human spirit. The first awareness is generated in the belief that prior generations failed to conserve "nature"—that is to say, the world outside of man; the second in the belief that they failed to protect nature within us, or human nature. The sort of violence to land and life of which man is peculiarly capable is regarded as wrong because it is counter-evolutionary to our species.

The wildlife crisis is part of a larger environmental crisis which, in turn, is a twentieth-century collision between supply and demand: the supply of earthly resources and the demand of a people growing ever more numerous, more wasteful, and more untidy. The crisis was predictable; it did not result from some new factor such as men's losing faith in their gods. What is new is the public awareness. *Time* magazine identified the environmental crisis as a point in history when, on August 1, 1969, it began to contain a new section called "Environment." In 1970, other national magazines printed whole issues or special supplements: *Life*, "Ecology, a Cause Becomes a Movement" (68:3); *Look*, "Earth Day, April 22—The Fight to Save America Starts Now" (34:8); *Newsweek*, "The Ravaged Environment" (75:4); *Ramparts*, "Ecology Special" (8:11); *Saturday Review*, "Environment and the Quality of Life" (53:10); and *Scientific American*, "The Biosphere" (233:3).

On Earth Day, the phrase "environmental teach-ins" became part of the English language. By the year 1970, the message was coming clear to all who listen: We can never hope to "get away" from earth and from ourselves.

All of us see changes in buildings, cities, automobiles, clothing, and other trappings of civilization, but few see changes in the biosphere of the world, for these are subtle and obscure. Changes in material culture fluctuate with fashion, while changes in the biosphere have a way of becoming deep and final. It was the naturalists, from career scientists of the Barry Commoner and Garrett Hardin breed to organic gardeners, bird-watchers, and a great many hunters, who early saw the important changes and who are now so deeply disturbed at the degradation of wildlife environments.

The bald eagle, the bird that stands for the United States of America, is in trouble. Outside Alaska, only 5,000 are left. The California condor, the largest land bird in America, has been reduced to 50 individuals nesting in one mountain range. About 50 whooping cranes and somewhat over 1,000 trumpeter swans are alive in the wild. The grizzly bears of the United States outside Alaska number about 1,500, and the wolves are down to 1,000.

I have suggested that the new attitudes originated in concerns both for wild animals and for humanity. The latter proposition,—that the fate of the animal is the same as the fate of man himself, is an abstraction, not easy to prove by argument. Yet I believe that many of us today are taking a deeper look at inner feelings. We are wonderstruck by the image of our lonely world as seen from eternal space, and we fear that we may lose this tiny ball of beauty through failure to appreciate it. As we launch the first spacecraft to leave the solar system (Pioneer 10), we fasten upon it a goldplated message telling in cryptic marks that at least one Man and one Woman survive on the third planet out from Sol.[3] Between the lines of this celestial advertisement is there a note of apprehension? Do we fear that our easy willingness to destroy may leave no sentient being to send a later message to the stars?

In our new self-awareness, we look at the wild animals of earth and we see them plain—they are blood relations. We are increasingly reluctant to kill them except for subsistence or to protect ourselves.

More directly, this new morality deals with the ways that animals should, and should not, be used. At one extreme, a creature is said to be useful if it brings pleasure to those who, though they can never hope to see it in the flesh, are satisfied to know that it is out there somewhere in the wild—free, alive, hidden, breathing, continuing its ancestral bloodline. At the other extreme, a creature is said to be put to its highest use when it is converted to pet food, or when its cured remains are draped on a human body for the satisfaction of personal vanity. I will try to show, not that a particular use is intrinsically right or wrong, but that some uses fit better than others into the new morality.

The symbolic animals in the wildlife revolution—
the emblems on the banners of the marchers—are the
whale, wolf, eagle, falcon, and other creatures that
breathe deeply the airs of freedom. At the Stockholm
conference, hundreds took part in a whale march, following a truck draped in black plastic to resemble a
whale. The city of Duluth has established the Hawk
Ridge Nature Reserve where hawks can be seen as they
soar cleanly above the waters of Lake Superior. School-
children in 1971 flooded congressmen with letters de-
manding that wild horses be protected from "villainous"
dog-food makers and "heartless" cattlemen who "want to
keep all the grass for their cows." [4] A group of young
people from the University of California recently came
to see me because they were eager to study the behavior
of whales, seals, or dolphins. They wanted no part in on-
going, million-dollar, military research upon marine
mammals, and they were lukewarm about studying
animals in commercial aquariums. They were trying to
articulate more than a scientific curiosity about wild
animals; they were trying to say, "We care."

Each one of the symbolic animals is adapted to its
place and style of life; each moves in perfect accord with
nature. We humans have forgotten how so to move, and
yet the animal is in us; wild creatures are other kinds of
people; they contain the roots of mankind in bodies
which have taken another evolutionary course.

"I love forms beyond my own," says the naturalist-

Introduction

poet Loren Eiseley, "and regret the borders between us." [5]

≽

In the present book, the word nature means the earth without man. (There is no such place, yet the word is useful.) Environment means the real earth including the only animal which has tried to subdue it. Wildlife means birds and mammals, except for domestic animals and common pets. The setting of the book is principally, though not exclusively, the United States. I frequently cite examples of wildlife management in my home state of Washington. The "new conservationist" will appear often in these pages. He/She is an imaginary person whom I have built from study of opinion in outdoor magazines, humane society newsletters, wildlife conservation journals, the national press, the voices of my students and colleagues in wildlife biology, and from personal reflection. He/She is close to what economist George R. Hall identified a decade ago as the "naturalist-conservationist." Hall foresaw a struggle shaping up between the technological conservationists, concerned with goals of efficiency, maximum yield, and avoidance of "waste," and the naturalist-conservationists, concerned with trying to change consumer tastes. [6] I have identified myself, deservedly or not, with the new conservationists, with a special concern for their probing questions: What are the acceptable limits to the killing of wild animals? Where lie the moral boundaries?

Chapters 1 to 9 of the book contain a sampling of confrontations between people and wildlife which illustrate pleasant encounters as well as conflicts of interest. These show how people help and harm wild animals, and how the habits of wild animals are helpful and harmful to people. Examples are drawn from sport-hunting, trapping animals for their skins, controlling animal pests, and other activities, discussion of which is continually shaping the wildlife ethic.

In all the world, over a million species of animals, from microscopic, one-celled sparks of life to man himself, have been named and described. Collectively they represent a mass of 2 million million tons, of which the bodies of men, women, and children contribute one part in 10,000.[7] Though the human fraction is tiny, the interplay between the people and the remainder of the biomass is complex beyond understanding. People and animals do things to one another, causing people to classify animals as good or bad, and their own reactions toward animals as right or wrong.

The late Ernest P. Walker, assistant director of the National Zoo for more than twenty-five years, would now and again eavesdrop on visitors at the zoo as they stared at some unfamiliar beast in a cage. "What good is it?" they would ask. Or, "Is it mean?"[8] Such questions are not really vacant; they represent a fumbling effort of the human to understand the animal. The visitor looks at the beast with feelings which range from embarrassment to fear and tries to bring it into focus where he can appreciate it. He hopes his questions will be answered: "It is useful to man because . . ."; "No, it is never mean." The visitor cannot see across the 10 million years that separate him from his nearest relative in Old Africa; he does not understand that all beasts are amoral.

To be sure, we tend to label creatures: the bobwhite quail as good all of the time, the fox as good most of the time, the starling as bad most of the time, and the vampire bat as bad all of the time. This is not a useful habit. The words beneficial and injurious are properly applied, not to species, but to populations at a specific time and place. A few beavers in an aspen glade are welcome for the good they do by storing water and by delighting visitors to their ponds; a hundred may be unwelcome for the harm they do by overcutting the food supply and eroding the stream banks. A few porcupines in an evergreen forest may give pleasure to the traveler along the trail at dusk; many porcupines mean trouble for the forester, who sees the girdled and dying tops of the trees they have fed upon.

Our attitude toward wildlife is influenced also by the level of human population. The more people, the more intense the competition for uses of wildlife and the louder the arguments over what is use and what is abuse. As the population of America burgeons, we are beset by problems of multiple use of land versus special, or dominant, use. How do we decide the optimum use of a tract of land or water that offers many simultaneous uses? The phrase multiple use has a fine, democratic sound but is often employed by logging, mining, and water-power interests to justify penetration of beautiful wild regions that have greater value when left alone.

On the California coast, north of Santa Cruz, lies Año Nuevo Island, a treeless rock which once supported a lighthouse. When the island was abandoned, proposals were made to turn it over for conventional park use by hikers, sightseers, and sportsmen, but the State of California wisely chose to make it a special preserve open exclusively to programmed visits. Now it is a treasure-house of wildlife, supporting thousands of Steller sea lions, California sea lions, elephant seals, and harbor seals. It is open to any citizen who understands its precious qualities and who agrees to abide by its rules. "It was taken out of service," complained a man in Santa Cruz. In fact, it was not, and though he could not see this, perhaps his children can.

In the field of biology there are scholarly books which classify the uses of wildlife as consumptive (or extractive) and nonconsumptive—which is only to say that at times a man will kill or capture an animal and at other times will stand afar, "using" the animal without harming it. The classification is academic, for though it describes the impact of the man on the animal it says nothing about the recoil on his own conscience. As a rule, consumptive use, or harvesting, of wildlife has only a temporary effect on the stock, whereas consumptive use of a spiritual resource can be devastating.

Discussion of any confrontation between people and wildlife today is apt to cause semantic irritation, which is not bad in itself but rather is like the itch of a healing wound. The people-wildlife relationship is under examination in the light of the new conservation, and those involved are finding new words for old situations and old words for new ones. Some time ago, on a visit to the Pribilof Islands (the fur seal islands) of Alaska, I was puzzled to see that the agent in charge of the sealing workers had issued sweatshirts stenciled with the words SEAL PRUNER. By this device he was trying to show the public that only "surplus" seals are subtracted from the herd, for its own good.

Part Two of the book describes the working machinery of wildlife management—that is, the everyday process of coping with the neds of wild animals and of people in a changing nation. Wildlife management is an art, a science, a business, and a professional operation. Its structure is centered in the state game departments and its work is supported by several thousand public agencies and private groups. As a formal operation, it is rather recent. The first American professional society in the field, the Wildlife Society, was founded in 1937, and the first American textbook on wildlife management was published in 1948.[9]

Some new conservationists object to the word management because of its overtones of manipulation and of routine killing of animals which have no say in their own fate. It is presumptuous, they claim, for us to think we can solve for animals their population problems when we cannot solve our own. I agree that management has often meant little more than restraint on killing. The faint odor of the process will not be cleared by sanitizing its name, however, but only by improving its machinery in order to make its products more widely acceptable to all members of society. Some are even annoyed by the word resource as applied to living animals. It does indeed suggest a utility, or an inert material that can be chopped, dug, or burned, but it also means (according to one dictionary) "something that can be turned to for support or help." I like this definition.

In dealing with management, I touch very lightly on the fate of rare and endangered species, for I have no words which can reach those persons who would let a species go. A colleague has said what many of us think: "Perhaps the best nonemotional reason for seeking to retain a few species is for the practice it may give us in picking what should be saved. If man cannot save the bald eagle and other frills, it follows that he will never be able to save himself. It is not much of a jump from making a choice among species to making a choice among racial, religious, or economic groups." [10] Of the forty-one species of birds and mammals native to the United States exterminated in historic time, eighteen have been lost during the present century.

The third and final part of the book is mainly de-

Introduction

voted to predictions of changes that will occur in wild-life management, assuming that the new conservationists will rise to the top in government and in the social-power groups that influence government. The predictions are the basis of a future ethic toward wildlife.

PART ONE

CONFRONTATIONS BETWEEN PEOPLE AND WILDLIFE

 CHAPTER 1

Shooting for Sport

WHEN the United States Bureau of the Census counted our heads in 1970 it also interviewed people selected at random who met the specifications of "substantial hunter." These were individuals twelve years old and older who hunted on at least three days or spent at least $7.50 on hunting in 1970. Hunting in the United States turns out to be a mighty important sport. More than 14 million hunters spent $2 billion on guns, guides, dogs, food, lodging, transportation, licenses, privilege fees, and other prerequisites of the chase. They spent $136 million on food and $51 million on alcoholic beverages—a diet in balance with the hazards of the hunt. In an average of twelve trips during the year, the average hunter pursued small game (mainly rabbits, squirrels, pheasants, and doves) 61 percent of the time, big game (mainly deer and elk) 27 percent, and waterfowl (mainly ducks and geese) 12 percent.[1]

Confrontations between People and Wildlife

During the decade 1960–1970, about one in ten Americans aged twelve and older—one in five men and one in eighty women—was a substantial hunter. The census data indicate that participation in hunting dropped a little over the decade.[2] The following figures are for substantial hunters in the United States:

	1960	1970
Number of hunters	14,637,000	14,336,000
Percent hunters in comparable		
U.S. population	11.2	9.2
Percent hunters, male	21.7	18.3
Percent hunters, female	1.5	1.1

But according to data furnished by the state game departments, hunters *increased* during the decade. Figures for all persons of all ages in the United States show 13,902,578 paid hunting license holders in 1960; 15,370,481 in 1970.[3]

In a business analysis prepared for *The New York Times,* Marylin Bender writes that "firearms and ammunition rank third among the five slowest growing categories [of sporting goods]."[4] This is perhaps an indication that sport-hunting is nearing a plateau.

Though statisticians can estimate the numbers and characteristics of hunters in the United States, they seem unable to tell us much about the hunted. No agency or private group compiles the game-kill records of the fifty states. In view of the fact that the federal government returns to the states millions of dollars collected from taxes on sporting goods, one would think that the government might demand a game-kill return from every state. The government does in fact gather data on the kill of native big game animals and on the kill of waterfowl. I have tabulated those data, adding an estimate of the kill of doves.[5]

Kill of big game animals	
Mammals *	2,247,000
Turkeys	137,533
Kill of waterfowl (ducks, geese, and coots),	
retrieved and unretrieved †	19,550,000
Kill of mourning doves	20,000,000

* Antelope, bear (black and grizzly), bison (semiwild), caribou, cougar, deer (black-tailed, mule, and white-tailed), elk, goat, moose, peccary, and bighorn sheep. Deer and elk account for 94 percent of the total killed.

† About 82 percent of waterfowl were retrieved.

I find only fragmentary data on the millions of small game mammals, shorebirds, and upland game birds killed in the United States. A conservative estimate of all animals killed by sports-hunters yearly is: mammals, 5 million–10 million; waterfowl, 20 million; land birds, 40 million; total 65 million–70 million.

☙

As I visualize the 14 million hunters of America I see, at one extreme, the farm boy with his .22 rifle, moving along in the sun and shadow of the cottonwoods, the cool dust of autumn spurting between his toes. One hour and two squirrels later, he comes home to Mom, who fries his game in cornmeal for his supper. At the other extreme, I see the big-game hunter pictured in color in the lastest sporting magazine, clinging to a wilderness ridge in the Yukon, sighting his rifle on a bighorn sheep. He has saved for a year to make this trip, which will cost him $2,000 and two weeks' time.

I open the *American Rifleman,* a journal received by a million members of the National Rifle Association, and regard with wonder a picture of a little boy held upon the body of a dead deer by his smiling mother, Peg, while Ed, the smiling father, holds the Mannlicher-Schonaeur .30-06 with which he overcame the beast. In the story, entitled "Family Plan Hunting," Ed tells how he gave Peg a shotgun for an engagement present. After marriage, they scrimped to buy an extra rifle. Now Peg has become "a woman who believes that children should be brought up in the outdoor traditions of their forefathers." [But how distant those in time?] Ed believes that "there are no eyes as big as those of a little boy with one hand wrapped around an antler, helping drag a buck in over wet, fall leaves. . . . We have tried to teach our children to respect all life, but to take a matter-of-fact attitude toward the taking of game animals. We do not dwell upon death, but rather concentrate on the idea that this buck will provide us some wonderful meals this winter." [6]

All hunters like to follow in imagination the high

adventures of the Eds and Pegs out there in the good ole mountains, but the hunting stories today are not what they used to be; they are too instructive.

❧

WHAT are the motives of the sportsman? Why does the average American hunter spend $150 a year on his avocation?

In the first place, I think, the hunter wants to be free —to escape for a little while from the routine of the daily job, the petty chores around home, and the social obligations of the family man. In defending his hobby he will often speak of freedom, or of his right to hunt. Hunting is therapeutic. When he is out there in the sunshine he is re-created and cleansed; his senses are washed with natural beauty.

He wants to belong—to be recognized as a member of a ceremonial group, to sit around the fire at dusk with fellows who have come together for a common purpose, leaving all class distinctions behind. The trophy of the hunt, whether it is a five-point set of antlers or only the privilege of saying "I got my limit," is the badge of membership in the group. At its extreme, this reason for hunting is pure machismo, and the gun, according to some psychologists, is an extension of male anatomy. (There are, in fact, fifteen male hunters to every female.)

He loves the matériel of the chase—the bright red shells, perfect in shape and order, the walnut stock rubbed to the feel of his hand, the slender tripod that steadies his rifle for a cleaner shot at the game, the floppy hat flecked with the blood of old triumphs, and the $50 boots wafting the odor of pine tar. I will not try to explain this attachment for solid things. Truth to tell, I share it myself. Is it perhaps a vestige of a hoarding instinct that long ago meant survival to the race? Among the vertebrates, only certain birds and mammals cache food for later use. The lower, cold-blooded fishes, amphibians, and reptiles live entirely in time present. For the good of mankind, I trust that the possessive instinct will take us on an evolutionary course toward the storing of ideas, rather than objects.

An argument often presented is that the hunter is playing a predestined role. He is the caveman defending his loved ones from the savage beast. The prehistoric humanoid was a hunter and killer; the predatory instinct still runs in our blood—or so goes the argument. Never mind that modern hunting with the help of man's technology is very different from primitive hunting. Never mind that behaviorists discredit the inheritance of agressiveness and that human teeth are not the teeth of a carnivore. A sense of rightness about hunting is for some hunters equivalent to religion, and for a nonhunter to challenge that faith is a waste of time. Yet, for too many hunters, the metallic feel of a gun—a solid extension of personal power—is a temptation to kill carelessly. Ten short-eared owls, wounded by shot, were brought to the Audubon Wild Bird Clinic near my home last fall during the hunting season. If the man who shot them had been asked to kill them with a stick, he would have demurred. With a gun in his hand, the hunter is remote from his prey and his conscience. Those little birds were my owls and I resent the arrogance behind their death.

Some contend that the hunter is doing a kindness to animals by thinning their populations, thereby releasing more food and shelter for the individuals that escape his gun. Were they exposed to the "cruelty" of nature, some fraction of the weaker and unluckier members would die each year of starvation, exposure, or accident. Better, says the shooter, to kill cleanly by bullet and reduce the sum total of suffering.

The death rate among wild animals is indeed high, with or without the intervention of man; no wild animal dies of old age. (An estimated 250,000 ducks died in one year on Great Salt Lake from a botulin poison which can develop naturally in stagnant mud.) The hunter will argue that his gun takes many individuals which would otherwise have died slowly and painfully, and of course this is true.

In addition, game animals sometimes increase to numbers harmful to man's interests and even to their own wild habitats. Those situations are most common where man has put the animals into some sort of artificial bind. I suggest that the first remedy considered should be restoration of the habitat to a condition as nearly natural as possible. If, for economic or political reasons, that cannot be done, shooting is the answer. The diplomatic approach, so to speak, ought to be tried before the military.

It is necessary here to keep in mind the distinction between compassion for an individual animal and regard for the species of which it is a temporary part. In the march of evolution the individual does not count. Though not one of us likes to see a rabbit suffer in winter or be torn by a fox, the thoughtful among us will see events of that kind as natural scenes in the drama of life. The survivors are a biological elite. Under primitive conditions, the hunter pursuing a band of deer eliminated selectively those individuals that lagged behind in the chase; the effect was a strengthening of the prey species. Now the effect is reversed, for if the hunter is allowed only one deer per season, he will tend to wait for one in prime body condition.

The most common game birds in the United States are mourning doves, numbering about 140 million at their peak in summer. I have heard game managers argue that the shooting of doves is helpful—or at least not harmful—to the species. Before the arrival of the next summer they say, 80 million of the original stock will die of natural causes and 20 million will be shot. Because the kill by hunters is thus only one-fifth of the total annual loss, and because dove hunting is a popular sport, it can be encouraged in the public interest. However, the dove population in the United States is now at its lowest level since 1954, when the federal government first undertook to estimate it. No one can prove that sport-shooting is implicated, and no one can prove that it is not. The State of Wisconsin has shoved the whole biological argument aside. In 1971 it classified the dove as a protected songbird and as the official state symbol of peace.

The hunter is said to be a powerful force in conservation of wildlife. This argument contains some truth and is very persuasive, though it calls for critical examination. By the political voice of 14 million hunters and the economic thrust of their $2 billion a year, many square miles of land and water have been preserved in wild and lovely condition. At the same time, the populations of many hunted species have increased to levels far higher than in pioneer days. The hunter points with pride to the historic contributions made by American sportsmen to restoration of wild turkey, white-tailed deer, antelope, and bison. He tells his story honestly, though he seems unaware of his egocentric position. It is fortunate that the needs of deer and ducks coincide with the desires of sportsmen. A man can really "help" a species only by insuring the natural selection that maintains its vitality. (He can of course undo some of the harm that he has already done it.) He can learn to appreciate its right to live and can study ways of sparing it harm.

The self-image of the hunter with respect to conservation was put in capsule form in President Richard M. Nixon's message of May 2, 1972, proclaiming the first National Hunting and Fishing Day:

"Through a deep personal interest in our wildlife resources, the American hunter and fisherman have paved the way for the growth of modern wildlife management programs. In addition, his purchase of licenses and permits, his payment of excise taxes on hunting and fishing equipment, and his voluntary contributions to a great variety of conservation projects are examples of his concern for wildlife populations and habitat preservation.

"His devotion has promoted recreational outlets of tremendous value for our citizens, sportsmen and non-sportsmen alike. Indeed, he has always been in the forefront of today's environmental movement with his insistence on sound conservation programs."

The historic contribution made by sport-hunters does deserve recognition. During the infancy of the wildlife movement in America, from 1900 to 1930, growing numbers of sport-hunters united in opposing the plumage hunters, the meat-hunters who supplied quail and duck to the city restaurants, the village sports who shot nighthawks in the public square for fun, and the greedier members of their own fraternity. As recently as 1933, 6 million bushels of corn were spread on the fields of Illinois to lure waterfowl within range of hunters in private gun clubs.

Gun and ammunition companies also were active in the early war to save wildlife and are still involved—in their own special ways—with conservation education. T. Gilbert Pearson, one of the first directors of the Audubon Society tells how he was approached in 1911 by the Winchester Repeating Arms Company (now Winchester–

Western Division of Olin Corporation) to become director of a new organization to preserve game birds and
mammals from overkilling. Pearson's salary was to be
doubled—from $3,000 to $6,000 a year. He declined but,
out of the discussion, the American Game Protective and
Propagation Association was created by a coalition of
arms manufacturers. They offered the young Audubon
Society $125,000, which also was declined.[7]

Prince Philip of England, himself a hunter, is amazed
"that so many townspeople seem to be incapable of understanding that hunting and conservation are now
compatible. . . . They simply will not, or do not wish to
recognize that in most parts of the world the leadership
in conservation has come from experienced hunting
sportsmen."[8]

Statements of this kind fail to impress the people
who are less interested in the history of wildlife conservation than in how it can be shaped to fit a new morality.
These say, for example, that acquisition of our national
wildlife refuges through a tax on sportsmen was simply
a mistake. Now all the refuges have been legally opened
to shooting, and the nonhunters—the bird-and-beast
watchers—have little hope of obtaining comparable lands
anywhere at any price.

Today sport-hunters face a growing crisis of con-
fidence and identity. Angry and defensive, they prevailed
on President Nixon to inaugurate National Hunting and
Fishing Day. The outdoor editor of my hometown paper

believes that celebration of the new day will brighten the image of the sportsman, who, he says, "has borne the brunt of vicious attacks from a new and growing breed of city cat that views hunting and the hunter with loathing."[9] When, in 1972, *Outdoor Life* printed a three-part series in vigorous defense of sport-hunting, the publisher called it perhaps the most important story to appear in that magazine in seventy-five years.[10]

As a hunter grows older, his vision of the man-wildlife relationship often changes in a way that foreshadows a similar change in American thought as it too matures. The American author Robert F. Leslie, after a hunter killed an orphan cub which he was mothering, wrote bitterly: "All hunting, except for survival, is a shabby postponement of growing up."[11] I knew an old forester who was wholly content to go hunting for elk amid the golden aspens in fall, unconcerned whether he did or did not kill one.

❧

THE argument between the hunters and the nonhunters of America continues unabated. What are the opinions of leaders in public thought about wildlife?

The National Audubon Society has taken a position on sport-hunting with which many in the new conservation movement will agree. "Since its origin at the turn of the century, the Society has never been opposed to the hunting of game species if that hunting is done ethically and in accordance with laws and regulations designed to prevent depletion of the wildlife resource. . . . But we do not advocate hunting. This is no contradiction, though some people seem to think it is. Our objective is wildlife and environmental conservation, not the promotion of hunting. We think lots of the justifications for hunting are weak ones, and too often exaggerated for commercial reasons, and we do not hesitate to say so when the occasion calls for it. But this does not make us anti-hunting. We are pushing people to think more clearly about these problems." [12]

The American Humane Association "is not opposed to regulated hunting . . . when individual species populations and trends, food and space requirements, and other natural mortality factors indicate that such population reductions are in the best interests of that species. [Our] only mandate is that such hunting, killing, cropping, harvesting or reduction be performed in the most humane, efficient and effective manner reasonably and practically available." [13]

This statement contains two salient points. First, a population may be thinned by killing when it becomes destructively abundant. Second, the thinning must not (by implication) entail the use of toys, such as bow and arrow, or hobby approaches, such as trophy selection, which cloud the purpose of the operation.

One of the leading spokesmen for wildlife conservation in America is A. Starker Leopold, a professor of forestry and biology at the University of California and son of pioneer conservationist Aldo Leopold. His understanding of the interplay between people and wild animals is both philosophical and practical. Recently asked for his views on hunting, he replied that it is "my favorite form of recreation." Then he made two valuable points: killing is incidental to the reason for hunting and it declines in importance in the mind of the hunter as he grows older. "I think that all of us start out as pretty bloodthirsty young hunters who want something in the bag. We later come to appreciate that the enjoyment of hunting is something quite apart from the killing. I'm not saying that you shouldn't be hunting birds. The point is that you're out there for the joy of the whole experience, and the shooting is secondary." [14]

When my neighbor, Freddy, was six years old, he was taken to see the Walt Disney movie *Olympic Elk*. On leaving the theater he said, "Gee! I'd like to hunt elk." "But why would you want to kill them?" inquired his mother, and he replied quickly, "Oh, I don't mean *kill* them, I mean *hunt* them!"

The president of the Wildlife Management Institute urges that more attention be given to the "public-acceptance factor." He says that "some people plainly are against blood sport and little probably can be done to change their views. They will not respond to explanation." But the others among the 155 million nonhunters who are merely "indifferent to hunting" can, he believes, be led to understanding if wildlife management is improved. Game management agencies must insist, by law if necessary, that all hunters behave like sportsmen. Tighter regulations are needed. Very few states, for example, penalize a shooter who kills or harms another. "Gun goons and outdoor rowdies are giving hunters and hunting a black eye. We must shape them up or ship them out." Wildlife agencies must recognize the need for specialists in human relations who can ease the tension between private landowners and the hunter-invaders.[15]

Russell E. Train, administrator of the Environmental Protection Agency, deplores "indiscriminate shooting, a result of literally hundreds of thousands of firearms in the hands of untrained and unconcerned vandals. If you would argue that shooting is not a significant factor in wildlife depredation, count the bullet holes in road signs the next time you drive to your favorite hunting area."[16]

I SOMETIMES wonder about the language of hunting. I question whether "game" or "sport" should be used to describe an activity in which one of the players has only his pure wildness to call on for defense, while the other has weapons of shocking power, lures and decoys, a hunting dog, telescopic vision, the automobile or boat, the ambush or blind, and a colored map of the migratory path of the prey. It is a game in which the stakes are life and death, but for only one of the players. It is a game in which courage is rarely called upon.

I believe that the sport-killing of wild animals, as

compared with sensing them in many other ways, is un-imaginative, though I do not quarrel with it as long as it does not infringe the rights of nonhunters. In the past, hunting has decimated species of birds and mammals, and the element of sport is still apparent in the activities of the man-packs who are riding down the last of the North American wolves and cougars. Hunting still shatters the quiet of the autumn hills and marshes, annoying and endangering the hiker who visits the outdoors in hunting season. The local game department disturbs the native faunas by planting exotic species of birds and mammals. Two million to 3 million ducks die annually from lead poisoning after they ingest shot scattered upon American wetlands. Sportsmen kill the wild carnivores and raptors, fascinating elements of our fauna, because these feed in part upon game. Game managers, using bulldozers, chains, and herbicides, clear the wild and beautiful scrublands of the Southwest to provide more food for deer. Some citizens will claim that hunters are more apt than nonhunters to cut fences, trample crops, destroy signs, and leave litter behind, though this slur on the sporting fraternity would be hard to prove.

At the age of sixty-odd, I do not understand why anyone should want to shoot an 8-ounce mourning dove or a clapper rail simply because the bird is a moving target and the test of a man's quickness on the draw. I do not understand how anyone, for pleasure, should want to take particles of life from the common good, the common trust.

Odd Ways of Hunting

WITHIN the law, the American hunter can choose among many weapons, many ways of stalking his prey, and many target species. When he hunts for deer in a thick forest he may be required to use short-range ammunition that will not endanger other hunters. He may not hunt deer with a small-bore rifle that cripples more often than it kills. He may not go after ducks with a rifle, or with a shotgun capable of firing more than three charges in rapid succession. The privilege of shooting from a boat, land vehicle, or aircraft has gradually been taken from him. Nonetheless, he is still allowed to hunt by certain odd methods just for the hell of it.

Some states allow hunting with hand guns or with Revolutionary War weapons—old-time muzzle-loading rifles using black powder and ball shot. The use of live, released pigeons for target practice is banned only in about fifteen states.

Confrontations between People and Wildlife

Some states condone the use of tethered birds in sporting competitions known as "turkey shoots." For eighteen years, a service club in a midwestern state put on a turkey shoot in autumn to raise money for charity. The shoot in 1970 was attended by 10,000 people, many of whom paid a dollar each to fire a gun at a living turkey tied by one leg, its body protected by a bunker and its head propped up in view by a forked stick. The birds were lined abreast in thirty-nine shooting lanes. Anyone, including children, could try to kill them. Some birds were frightened or wounded and broke legs or wings in an effort to escape. Local humane organizations protested for years against the shoots. The president of the club defended them, protesting that the turkeys did not know they were targets and the shooters could see only the head of the bird, and listing a number of worthy causes which were benefited by the shoots. However, the 1970 shoot was the last. The international office of the service club ordered the local club to cease and desist, under threat of losing its charter, and in 1971 the state passed a law forbidding the use of all captive animals as living targets.

Bow hunting with sharp, steel-tipped arrows is said by its 800,000 enthusiasts to be on the increase in the United States. Even the largest of game species, the Alaska brown bear, has been brought down by archery. The federal government allows bow hunting on many of its public lands, including the 40-mile-long Land Between the Lakes of the Tennessee Valley Authority.

Odd Ways of Hunting

Here fallow deer, a European import, may be hunted under elaborate restrictions—no crossbows, no indulgence in drugs or alcohol, no permanent shooting stands in the treetops, no blazing of trails, no all-terrain vehicles, no fires or spotlights, and no hunting from "domestic animals." The meaning of domestic animal is not clarified. I suppose it covers any mount imaginable to a Tennessee hunter.

As compared to a bullet, an arrow kills more slowly —by hemorrhage—and is therefore more cruel. Many wounded deer go bounding away to die unseen and unrecorded. However, Keith C. Schuyler, archery expert, has no direct evidence that the rate of cripple-and-loss is higher from archery than from gunning. He does believe that "the recovery rate for archers is probably somewhat less for two reasons. First, the animal is more likely to move some distance after a fatal shot. Second, hunting is usually done when foliage is still heavy in autumn [in advance of the gunning season] and it is more difficult to trail and to find such animals." [1]

Mr. Schuyler's plea, "We ask to share the out-of-doors with others who may not understand what motivates us," [2] seems reasonable until I begin to sort out my own thoughts about weaponry. Then I conclude that, in the light of present knowledge, a gun in the hands of a careful hunter is the more certain and therefore more humane weapon for killing a deer. In feeling the pain of the deer surprised by the arrow I overlook the pleasure of the archer in his sport.

Confrontations between People and Wildlife

On the bitter plains of South Dakota men still a-hunting go for buffalo. Every winter, the Department of Game, Fish and Parks disposes of 200 bison by slaughter, and 300 by sale on the hoof. It issues permits at $500 each for the privilege of shooting one bison inside the fence of Custer State Park, and of taking the meat for personal use. The hunter travels with a guide by car. When he has killed his animal, a radio call back to headquarters brings a hoist truck and a flat-bed truck to pick up the prize.

Surely from some far, eternal hillside the faded eyes of Kit Carson look down in disbelief.

In North America, along with the disappearance of wild lands, the crowding of human populations, and the growing tolerance of artificial values in human life, there has risen a system of sport-hunting that depends on animals raised in pens and released on semiwild shooting preserves. The system depends almost entirely on birds—pheasants, quails, ducks, partridges, and turkeys. Mammals cannot be raised economically for this kind of put-and-take hunting, although in many states mammal stocks are released on open preserves to multiply at their own biological pace.

The number of controlled-shooting preserves in the United States is nearing 3,000 and is growing fast. The Winchester–Western Division of Olin Corporation compiled a 1972–73 directory of 418 public, daily-fee preserves, some of which offer both bird and mammal targets.[3] The North American Game Breeders and Shooting Preserve Association, a powerful trade association of business firms, and the 114-member group of industries known as the National Shooting Sports Foundation promote the sale of breeding stock, bird dogs, feeds, fencing, training films, short courses and books—even books on how to be an "outdoor writer." Visitors are encouraged to tour the model shooting preserves of Winchester–Western at Nilo Farms, in western Illinois, and those of the Remington Company at Remington Farms, Chestertown, Maryland.

High on the list of American sporting contests is the One-Shot Antelope Hunt, staged each year at Lander, Wyoming. Only six teams, each consisting of three men, are invited. These include astronauts, governors, tradebook editors, and other notables. After a blessing by a Shoshone chief, each man moves out with his rifle and a single round of ammunition. He has one chance; if he fails to kill, he will never again be invited to the One-Shot, though he can return periodically to target-shoot and fraternize with the old boys. I have just read a story in which the editor of *Field and Stream* tells of attending the latest One-Shot. It is a good story, and I find myself once again on the rolling tan prairies of the West in a wind that sings of a million years gone and a million years to come, and of the pine needles it has moved in passing, and of the spicy odors it has lifted from the sage. . . . "The range was 157 yards," concludes the editor; "the bullet had severed the spine." [4]

Some day I should like to be invited to a None-Shot Antelope Hunt.

For many hunters, the attraction of the sport is competition for trophy animals, which are the larger, finer, more symmetrical individuals in the population—the older animals that have escaped the guns of men as well as the hazards of nature. A book, *North American Big Game,* is the peerage of trophy heads, antlers, horns, skulls, or tusks of thirty-two kinds of mammals. It is published by the Boone and Crockett Club, an organization admired for its devotion to the principles of fair chase, though questioned for its obsession with trophy hunting. By its own statement, "The Club wishes to encourage the sportsman in selective hunting. The sportsman who will pass by a number of mediocre heads in his search for one of oustanding dimensions is doing more for conservation than he who is ready to shoot the first animal he encounters." [5]

This statement is questionable, to say the least. The trophy hunter may argue that older animals have done their duty as breeders and are surplus to the race. But survival into old age is evidence (though not proof) of genetic superiority and therefore a reason for sparing such animals. Wild animals are presumably able to breed as long as they continue in good health. Female fur seals begin to bear pups at three or four years of age and continue to bear until at least age twenty-two, beyond which few are alive for study.

Another nasty feature of "selective" hunting is that it encourages the unscrupulous hunter to abandon the body of a game animal he has killed if, soon thereafter, he spots a better specimen. A biologist working in a Utah national forest examined the bodies of 358 deer which had died of gunshot wounds and had not been recovered by the hunters. Expressed as "crippling loss in percentage of legal kill [within class]," the carcasses were bucks, 7 percent; does, 25 percent; fawns, 42 percent. "The study strongly indicated a rather high recovery by hunters of wounded bucks, but a very low recovery of antlerless deer [does and fawns]. Evidently this difference was in direct response to the premium placed upon the two classes of deer by the hunters," concluded the biologist.[6]

Beyond its effect on animals, trophy hunting dulls the meaning of human life. I have before me a taxidermist's catalog illustrating the "den" of a New Mexican hunter. On the floor are the skins of ten assorted creatures and on the wall the mounted heads of about thirty other sacrifices to vanity. To kill an animal for a conversation piece is indeed a sick and sad expression of human behavior. That message is plain enough in the glassy eyes of the Things who look down from the wall; it is read by young people in the new conservation movement but not by the hunter from New Mexico.

To kill all four of the main kinds of North American wild sheep (bighorn, desert, Stone, and Dall) is known in sporting circles as the Grand Slam, and those who achieve it are privileged to wear a shoulder patch and a gold pin. Jack O'Connor, shooting editor of *Outdoor Life*, made it about twenty-five years ago and now, having seen the "tremendous amount of lying, poaching, and

45

cheating" that competition for the Slam gives rise to, wishes that no one had thought of it.[7] The Grand Slam Club, faced with the evidence that a few of its members had broken federal and state laws in order to gain admission, asked them to resign.

John Steinbeck told a little story—a personal story as wine-dry as the hills of Baja California where it is laid. With a companion, he was resting in the shade while a couple of Indian friends scoured the hills for *borrego*, or bighorn sheep. He wrote that this is "the nicest hunting we have ever had. . . . We do not like to kill things —we do it when it is necessary but we take no pleasure in it." Toward evening, the Indians return without sheep but with solid evidence thereof. "On the way back from the mountain, one of the Indians offered us his pocketful of sheep droppings, and we accepted only a few because he did not have many and he probably had relatives who wanted them. . . . For ourselves, we have had mounted on a small hardwood plaque one perfect *borrego* dropping. And where another man can say, 'There was an animal, but because I am greater than he, he is dead and I am alive, and there is his head to prove it,' we can say, 'There was an animal, and for all we know there still is and here is the proof of it. He was very healthy when we last heard of him.' " [8]

Hunting any wild animal from aircraft was banned by the federal government in 1971, though a wide loophole remains. The law still allows this unsavory practice to continue where necessary for the "protection of land, water, wildlife [!], livestock, domesticated animals, human life, or crops." [9] The law was passed too late to save a thousand wolves shot from airplanes in Alaska in 1971. Under new game direction in Alaska, a ban on shooting wolves from aircraft went into effect in 1972.

The Defenders of Wildlife, an organization dedicated to the preservation of all forms of wildlife, maintains that aerial hunting is against Federal Aviation Administration regulations because it "involves acrobatic flying below prescribed altitudes [1,500 feet above the ground]; it involves in addition the use of an aircraft in such a manner as to endanger the lives of the pilot and the gunner." [10] This is an ingenious argument, though I feel sure many Defenders would prefer to see the case argued on plain grounds of humaneness.

The North Dakota Game and Fish Department tells in an article how one can lure a red fox within shooting range by blowing into a little gadget that mimics the voice of a rabbit in distress. It is best to blow *diminuendo,* says the article. "This closely follows the wild situation where a rabbit screams vehemently when first injured, gradually toning down, and then shortly before death utters a few loud short shrieks." [11] By this time you have that cunning old foxy devil right in where you can blast him.

Hunting with falcons, the sport of princes, is plummeting in America because the stock of wild peregrines is almost gone. In the 1940s the birds began to disappear, and only years later did biologists learn that agricultural pesticides, ingested in the bird's food, cause the female to lay eggs with abnormally thin shells. These collapse in the nest and the embryos die. Today, peregrines are extinct in all the North American East and the upper Mississippi Valley; they persist in diminishing numbers in the Far West and the North. Even those industrial chemists who pooh-pooh the dangers of DDT are quiet when confronted with the evidence of empty nests and silent cliffs. A fledgling falcon today is worth over $1,000 on the black market. A falconer from British Columbia (whose bird loft I once visited) was arrested in July 1970 in northern Quebec with twelve captured hawks. The birds were confiscated and he was fined $2,025.

Members of the Audubon Society in San Francisco recently took turns camping in a tent for eight weeks, guarding a falcon nest to protect the parent birds and their five young from poachers. They were successful, but volunteer wardens who watched a nest on Morro Rock, California, were less fortunate. Early in the spring of 1972, thieves stole the fledglings. After an appeal to members of a California hawking club, the babies were secretly returned—left in a bag at the base of the rock. Volunteer climbers put them back in the nest. Later in May, the birds were stolen again, and this time they were not returned.

The governments of the United States and Mexico signed an agreement in 1972 which gives protection from capture to all raptors (birds of prey), though it does not rule out their use in falconry.[12] Regulation of falconry is left to the states, any one of which can ban it altogether. The State of Washington issued 279 falconry permits in 1972. Birds held under permit were captured abroad, where capture is not illegal, or were taken in North America prior to March 10, 1972. The goshawk and red-tailed hawk are replacing the peregrine in popularity among falconers.

The catalog of a Florida pet-rancher lists nineteen species of hawks and hawk-eagles native to the New and Old World, offered for sale in 1973. "We do not stock any falcons from the United States," explains the rancher, "as we do not believe in exhausting our bird life here." [13]

Biologists have lately succeeded in hatching hawks bred by artificial insemination. Conceivably an endangered species could be held in protective custody until such time as DDT, widely banned on December 31, 1972, had dissipated from its environment. The new conservationists, however, are not enthusiastic about hawks in test tubes. They are concerned with the declining health of our civilization, of which dying hawks are only a symptom. They look to a future when political action will restore clean and safe places in which people, as well as hawks, can raise their young.

CHAPTER 3

Killing for Subsistence

SUBSISTENCE hunting is discussed here as a counterpoint to sport-hunting, not because it is very important in the United States. Indeed, all the meat-hunters in the world comprise only 0.003 percent of mankind. The percentage is even lower in the United States. In this country, by and large, we are well fed; we consume nearly twice as many food calories per capita as are consumed by the peoples of Asia, Africa, and Latin America. We spend little time scrounging in the wild for food; hunting for subsistence is largely pursued by Indians, Aleuts, and Eskimos.

In the village of Gambell, on St. Lawrence Island, in the Bering Sea, I have seen a bronze tablet that is bolted to the skull of a bowhead whale. It reads:

> Gambell has been designated a registered national historic landmark under the provisions of the Historic Sites Act of August 21, 1935. This site possesses exceptional val-

ues in commemorating or illustrating the history of the
United States. . . .

NATIONAL PARK SERVICE, 1961

The tablet marks the center of a sea-animal economy which was once critically important but is now
changing rapidly. Charles Brower of Point Barrow
(1863–1945) and Vilhjalmur Stefansson of the Arctic
(1879–1962) could say truthfully that they saw the
Stone Age Eskimo; [1] no living man can say it now. The
Eskimo-Americans of St. Lawrence still hunt for whales,
seals, and sea birds, though now they travel by snow-
mobile and by huge walrus-hide canoes powered by out-
board motors. They carry rifles, shotguns, and bomb-
lances. Supply ships and airplanes bring in most of their
food. They kill the walrus mainly for its hide and its
ivory tusks.

Native hunters in Alaska in 1971 took about 40
polar bears; sport-hunters using aircraft took 230. An
anthropologist who lived with the Eskimos at Wain-
wright, Alaska, in the late 1960s writes that: "Polar bear
hunting has been drastically reduced in recent years,
perhaps due to the rise of airplane hunting by wealthy
outsiders which, if nothing else, keeps the bears far out
on the pack ice. The Eskimos no longer go out every day
looking for bears, especially not on foot as they used
to." [2]

When I first went to the Pribilof Islands in 1940,
the native Aleut-Americans had little meat except what
they saved from the by-products of the sealskin harvest.

Now they eat boned beef, sold in stores which they own themselves. Fur sealing on the open ocean by North American natives, still permitted by law, reached its peak in 1925 with the taking of over 6,000 seals, about one-quarter of the entire harvest from the Pribilofs that year. Today the inquiring anthropologist will be lucky to find a sealing harpoon or canoe except in a museum.

The Marine Mammal Protection Act of 1972 acknowledges the rights in wildlife of natives, with certain restraints. Coastal resident Indians, Aleuts, and Eskimos may take marine mammals for subsistence or for the manufacture of "authentic native articles of handicrafts and clothing [if] the taking is not accomplished in a wasteful manner." Should the government in future determine that any stock is depleted, it can regulate the number of animals taken.[3] Lawyers are already complaining of vagueness in the words "wasteful" and "depleted," but at any rate the intent of the law is good.

In northern Canada, where many Eskimo families are dependent on caribou for food and fiber, the sustained harvest of 15,000 caribou is valued at $1,920,000 (based on the alternate cost of meat at $1 a pound). Under primitive conditions, each family needed 250 caribou a year; today, the need is 100 to 150.

Were the prehistoric aborigines of North America conservationists? In the sense of managers, no. They lived in regions where the animal-food supply was reasonably abundant. Their own numbers fluctuated with those of the wild animals. With the possible exception of fire deliberately set, they had no important means of manipulating the population level of any wild species, had they wished to do so. They were not stewards of wildlife, but though they did not practice conservation they felt it. They responded to the world around them as though they had predicted two modern definitions of conservation: "a state of harmony between men and land" and "a wise principle of co-existence between man and nature."[4] The aborigines were in, and of, nature; they studied nature for the survival value of its teachings. All things seen and unseen to them were real; there was no word in the primitive languages for "conservation" any more than there was a word for "politics" or for "art."

The North American Indian was wasteful, I suppose, when he stampeded bison over a "buffalo jump" in Wyoming and killed more animals than he intended. From the evidence of bones found today at the base of cliffs, he may have driven as many as 3,000 at a time. The Indian's reliance on wildlife was so absolute, however, that any deliberate departure from careful use of the resource would have been foolish and, in the eyes of the tribe, antisocial.

George Catlin wrote of a bloody affair in 1832 when a party of Sioux brought to a white man's encampment 1,400 fresh bison tongues, having left the bodies to rot. The Indians were after whiskey, which they duly received in trade for the tongues.[5] That affair does not prove that the Indian was wasteful; it only proves that an individual possessed of a white man's gun and a white man's thirst was a modified Indian.

Americans came very close to losing the bison. By

1889 the population had been reduced to 0.01 percent of its primitive size. Only 541 individuals were known to be alive.

To a sensitive person, the disappearance of an animal kind is a sadness in which part of his own life collapses. Twenty years ago, in a chilly pass of the Colorado Rockies far above timberline, I picked up the leg bone of a bison. It was crumbly and gray, covered with lichen growth. The beast of which it had been a part was perhaps one of that little band which held out in Lost Park until 1897. I balanced the bone in my hand for a while and thought of all the blizzards that had swept across the dying-place of the animal for half a century. I wondered whether any one of us—scientist, poet, or merchant—is more diminished than another by the loss of a species. Some day, perhaps, will mankind hunt down its own members, leaving a few near the end in a remote place where no young will be born? When Darwin wrote "survival of the fit" did he know that man, the newcomer, would redefine fitness so queerly that few other animals could survive without his consent? My thoughts evaporated in the sun and I put the bone in my haversack to be looked at again, as one would return to a relic of a martyr.

≱

I suppose that aboriginal rights and privileges in hunting in North America will disappear in time as the word aborigine loses its meaning. Intermarriage will blur physical differences between native and non-native, and, anyway, we all are aborigines. In the meantime, I believe that the treaty rights of the Indian, Aleut, and Eskimo should be respected for the good of those ethnic groups and for the good of the rest of us.

The problem of Indian fishing rights is very near to me in the Puget Sound of Washington. The commercial fishermen and the sport fishermen are set against the Nisqually people, who, under a nineteenth-century treaty, claim the privilege of netting salmon without regard to State law. In the controversy, buildings have been set afire, guns discharged in anger, fishnets cut, and men and women jailed. The American Friends Service Committee in a thoughtful book points out that "for the Indians of Puget Sound, salmon fishing is not a sport, nor is it merely a livelihood. It is an integral part of their way of life, and any tampering with their ancient fishing rights constitutes a threat to their cultural survival that goes far beyond the issues between conservationists and recreationists." The controversy seems to be quieting down through compromise. The protagonists are beginning to agree on separate and different approaches to the same fishery resource. "Diversity," say the authors of the book, "is the medicine for human survival." [6]

Hunting for subsistence and hunting for sport amount to the same thing in certain backwoods of America and in times when store-boughten beef is expensive. Deer poaching increases with the rising cost of beef. And sport-hunters everywhere bring to the table wildlife meat that contributes to the family food supply. To the best of my knowledge, no one has tried to estimate either the tonnage or the market value of the total wildlife killed in this country each year. Deer meat (venison) alone has been given a gross value of $80 million, though the net value is uncertain. What was the cost of obtaining the meat? Was it less than the alternate cost of buying beef? At this point one enters an economic thicket into which wildlife economists disappear from time to time, never again to be seen. The values of sport-hunting do not lend themselves to dollar analysis. One can estimate, however, that if hunters in the United States bring to the table each year 50 million birds and mammals (of the 65 million to 70 million they kill) and spend on hunting the $2 billion given in the census figures, their out-of-pocket cost per animal—whether it be dove or moose —is $40. That price suggests that the hunter should chew the meat slowly, meanwhile ruminating upon the fun he had in bagging it.

Some biologists believe that increasing attention will be given to experiments in replacing cattle, sheep, and goats now living on marginal grazing lands of North America with wild species more suitable to the vegetation and climate of those lands. The wool-bearing musk-ox is a candidate for colder regions; the African antelopes, especially eland and oryx, for hotter regions. Wild species, by and large, are more resistant to disease, more tolerant of weather extremes, and more efficient in their use of vegetation and water than are domesticated species which have been coddled, inbred for many generations, and often translocated to lands unlike their native homes. A wildebeest will gain daily 50 percent more live weight than an African cow of the same adult size; an impala will gain twice the live weight of an African sheep.

≥

I SOMETIMES wonder about our accepted practice of taking "crops" of wheat, pine trees, deer, or grouse from the land without putting anything back. Where will we come out in the end? The crops contain elements such as carbon, hydrogen, oxygen, and nitrogen, which can reach the land through air and water. They also contain elements such as sulfur, calcium, iron, and magnesium, which must come from the soil. Are minerals being released from the solid bedrock of earth and moving into the soil as fast as we are taking them away? Lacking provable answers to such questions, I shall continue wondering about man's extractive use of chemicals as compared with the use made by wild animals which defecate and die on the ground and return their substance there.

 CHAPTER 4

Killing for
the Fur Trade

ABOUT forty kinds of American mammals are called furbearers. Certain ones, like the black bear and fox, which
in one circumstance may do harm and in another good,
are changeably identified on game department lists as
furbearers, predators, game, or non-game endangered
species. The roster of American furbearers includes almost everything larger than a mouse that has hair:
badger, bassarisk, bears (grizzly, black, and polar), beaver, bobcat, cougar, coyote, ferret (nearly extinct), foxes
(cross, gray, red, and silver), lynx, marten, mink, muskrat, nutria (an immigrant from South America in the
1930s), opossum, otters (land and sea), raccoon, seals
(mainly fur seal and harbor seal; also bearded, ribbon,
and ringed seals and Steller sea lion), skunks (spotted

and striped), weasels (ermine and long-tailed), wolverine, and wolves (red and timber). Moles, squirrels, and wild rabbits and hares are seldom killed for the fur trade.

About 9 million furbearers—of which 92 percent are muskrat, nutria, or raccoon—are reported taken in the United States each year. Adding the unreported take would bring the total to more than 11 million. The dollar value of the fur trade is hard to estimate. Though the United States Government has, for several decades, been soliciting data from the individual states on their fur take, only forty states, not including the important fur state of Alaska, contributed information to the most recent federal report. Nonetheless, the killing of furbearers brings a primary revenue of at least $82 million a year.[1] The number of pelts and their dollar value breaks down as follows:

Produced in U.S.		
Wild furs	12.0 million	$47 million
Ranch furs	3.5 million	$35 million
Exported from U.S.		
All furs	14 million	$60 million

I do not know the number of trappers employed at the primary level of the trade. Perhaps 2,000 for each of the twenty-five important fur states, or a total of 50,000, would be a reasonable estimate for the United States.

The federal government offers data on the number of mink ranches (1,615 in 1971) but not on the number of fox ranches, which represent less than 1 percent of the mink ranches. The world production of ranch mink in 1971 was 21.5 million skins: Scandinavia, 9.3 million; Soviet Union, 6.0 million; United States, 3.5 million; Canada, 1.0 million; others, 1.7 million.[2]

According to the Fur Information and Fashion Council, American fur sales dropped from $365 million in 1965 to $293 million in 1971.[3] "The furriers wear a hunted look," says *Business Week* in reporting a threat to the American fur trade.[4] The industry is under attack by the new conservationists, who say that killing fur-bearers is harmful to animal populations and, what is more important, to human sensibilities. Some ask: If wild animals must be killed for their skins, how best can it be done humanely? while others ask, Should wild animals be killed for fashion in any circumstances? The heat of the controversy is indicated by the score of congressional bills and resolutions introduced at the turn of the 1970s dealing with rare and endangered species and with humaneness. Congress has not expressed itself on the ultimate morality of the fur trade, concluding perhaps that its legal obligation ends with defining (or trying to define) humaneness. Beyond lies the domain of private conviction.

Fur Age Weekly defends the fur trade with an eloquent statement called "A Furrier's Credo," by an anonymous but "very prominent member of the fur industry." It calls attention to the romance and dollar value of the fur trade throughout history and to the sane conservation ethic of the furrier. The credo ends: "I deplore the efforts of self-styled conservationists who hide behind assumed names and P.O. Box numbers, who play upon the emotions of well-meaning people of all walks of life and collect tens of thousands of dollar bills for their own self-aggrandizement, who account to no one for their efforts and seek to destroy the livings of many thousands of fine craftsmen citizens. If there is an endangered specie [*sic*] on the face of the earth, it is I." [5]

The wild-fur industry is defended, not only by the skin traders and processors, but by the trappers out in the bush. Members of the Fur Takers of America, a group organized in the middle 1960s, espouse a ten-point program which calls for inspiring "the ethics of true sportsmanship toward others who wish to enjoy the recreation and pleasure of the outdoors" and for setting up a "training program for our youth to teach them the necessity of true conservation." This program also calls for "good feeling, good will, and mutual understanding through a proper respect of the rights of the land owners." At its core is agreement "to oppose all laws or regulations which are biased or discriminatory to the Fur Takers of America." [6]

I find it hard to criticize the trapping fraternity, for among its members are individuals whom I regard as friends. I myself, in younger days, have trapped scores of animals without identifying myself as an agent of pain. Nonetheless, I wish the Fur Takers would be more open about their aims; would admit to being trappers in the business for money, not for moral leadership. I have a feeling that their constitution and bylaws would be improved by plain language. The trade might then be respected, if not endorsed, by the youth of the new conservation movement.

∌

THE populations of North American land furbearers are not threatened at the moment, thanks mainly to a falling demand for wild furs, but also to game departments that have banned the capture of endangered species and have restored, by translocation, live breeding stocks to depleted ranges. The wolverine and fisher, ghostly prowlers of the deep forest, are seen again in Idaho, Montana, and Oregon. There are only five fur bearers on the federal Rare and Endangered List—the eastern timber wolf, red wolf, San Joaquin kit fox, black-footed ferret, and Florida panther, or cougar.[7] Fur hunters played little part in pushing those five to the brink; the blame can be laid on government hunters engaged in killing predators and rodents, and on powerful "reclamation" agencies whose improvements have meant destruction for a good deal of wild America.

Serious (though I think unjustified) concern is now expressed for two marine furbearers of United States waters—the sea otter and the Alaska fur seal. More than 50,000 sea otters live along the coast of Alaska and about 1,000 along the coast of central California. Two hundred otters were recently moved from Alaska by airplane to beaches of British Columbia, Washington, and Oregon, where sea otters had been extirpated by hunters long ago. The State of Alaska began to crop sea otters in 1962 after a closed season of fifty-one years and by 1971 had taken nearly 3,000 skins. Discouraged by a poor market, the state has given up plans for regular cropping. The sea otters of California are well protected but are vulnerable to the first oil spill of unusual nastiness. Because the sea otter's pelage is among the silkiest of all mammals', containing 600,000 hairs per square inch, it can easily be fouled by an oily or gloppy substance, whereupon the otter dies of chill and exposure.

The story of fur-sealing is a Jack London story that never ends. It tells of men who wait in the fog . . . and when the fog lifts the men are gone. It tells of men who lie, cheat, and gamble for the possession of furs. It tells of the pride of Americans when Nat Palmer returned, one of the first men to see Antarctica—young Nat Palmer of Connecticut, hunting for seals in 1820. It tells of the shame of Americans in 1868 when the beaches of the Pribilof Islands of Alaska ran red with the blood of 300,000 seals.

And still in midsummer about 1,200,000 seals visit the Pribilof Islands to give birth. The main products of the fur seal industry are the rich pelts of the bachelor males three and four years old, valued at $4 million to $5 million a year.

The cropping of fur seals each year has a sparing effect, in theory at least, on 40,000 tons of fish and squid.

That effect is pleasing to commercial fishermen in the United States and also to those of Canada, Japan, and the Soviet Union—our partners in the North Pacific Fur Seal Convention. But while biologists can estimate the tonnage of seafoods eaten by seals, they have only a foggy notion of the real impact of the seals upon any commercial fishery. For example, fur seals are known to eat lampreys, which in turn are parasitic on salmon, so in the end the seals may actually be helping, rather than harming, the salmon fishery. An ecologist would put it this way: When you take a seal from the ocean, what kind of hole have you left?

On the Pribilof Islands, the records of a century show plainly that the present annual harvest of about 40,000 seals can be sustained. When pickets in Washington, D.C., called for an end to Pribilof sealing, *Audubon* magazine suggested that "well-meaning though their protest may have been, it was nonetheless without foundation from a conservation and biological viewpoint." [8]

But the new conservationists are looking beyond the bare fact of animal population size and the cliché that management has a salutary effect on the herd. We will grant you, they say, that in a controlled population the average seal gets a larger share of food, it grows fatter, and lives longer than it would in a free world without man. This is good for the individual but not necessarily for the species. When management softens the impact of natural forces, when it tries to make life easier for the seals, it quiets the very struggle for existence that has shaped these magnificent creatures over millions of years. It tampers with evolution in a way that could lead to a weaker genetic strain. Of this result no one can be sure, but likewise no one can be sure that management is biologically helpful, and statements to that effect are dishonest.

Jonas Salk, the developer of polio vaccine, has said approximately the same thing about the environment of mankind. "To free human life of antagonism, or resistance, adversity and therefore challenge, would be to deprive it of elements akin to food, which is part of the basic process essential to its fulfillment." [9]

≽

So much for biology; now the moral issue. The bachelor fur seals are killed by men born and trained on the Pribilof Islands. They drive the seals from the beaches to grassy meadows, where they select the bachelors. These they kill with a blow on the head from a heavy club, followed with a knife puncture through the heart. Six veterinarians who were invited to inspect the killing operations reported that "the current method of euthanasia . . . cannot be criticized from the standpoints of humaneness and efficiency; however, search for a method comparable in these respects and more aesthetically acceptable should be continued." [10]

There is another opinion, older by four hundred years—"The quality of mercy is not strained."

At any rate, killing fur seals on land is more humane than killing them at sea. The fur seal treaty of 1911 put an end to the bloody days of pelagic, or open sea, hunting. In those days the animals, many of them females bulging with unborn young, were shot indiscriminately, and many sank before they could be recovered.

The United States Department of Commerce, which now manages the fur seal herd, can be faulted for insisting upon a goal of optimum sustainable yield. This is good business, but, if we look at the record for the years 1956 to 1964, we see that an average of 25,000 female seals of breeding age were killed each year in order to reduce the size of the herd. And if we read between the lines, we may ask, What became of the suckling pups of those seals that were mothers? In fact, most of the pups died on the nursery, for a mother seal will rarely adopt another's young.

Now the final question of the moral issue: Should seals be killed for luxury under any circumstances? The new conservationists say no, because they draw the line between killing for need and killing for want. They do not deny an Alaskan native the right to kill a seal for food, but they question his right to kill to provide a thousand-dollar coat for a New York boutique.

Within the sealing controversy lies our human reluctance to think of the actual suffering or death of any animal, wild or domestic, though we are willing to use its product in our economy. Our kill-reluctance is graduated, lowest for bugs and germs, highest for mammals like ourselves, especially their females and young. An enterprising man proposed recently to raise and slaughter Dalmatian dogs for their attractive spotted pelts. He pointed out that it would be no worse than killing lambs in an abbatoir, but of course he was mobbed by dog lovers. "Human kind," says T. S. Eliot, "cannot stand very much reality." [11]

In an old trunk I find a Band of Mercy pledge that I signed fifty years ago in a school campaign, when I promised that I would "try to be kind to all harmless living creatures and try to protect them from cruel usage." Thus early in my training as a biologist I was put in the hard position of having to decide which animals were harmless and therefore to be treated kindly.

There is no place in new conservation thought for the old argument: Granted that the sealing business involves killing, it does employ a great many people. The number employed in any business is a poor index of its character.

Nor is there a place for the argument that sealing may be bad, but it is no worse than other kinds of killing. A biologist in the South African fur-sealing industry puts it this way: "Like other organisations associated with natural resouces, the sealing industry has not escaped the criticism that its activities are unnecessary, unimaginative and unethical. The protectionist attitude is somewhat puzzling when one considers the flimsy reasons for the various forms of death, legal or otherwise, inflicted by man on his own or other species." [12]

The same argument is pressed by those who condone the napalming of children in warfare—it's no worse than what the enemy is doing!

The methods of killing animals on fur ranches appear to be acceptably humane. Nonetheless, the editor of *Fur Trade Journal* advises fur-ranchers to "Beware visitors! . . . keep strangers out of your ranch," because the stranger might be a humane society "sniper" in disguise. "Even the most scientifically humane methods of killing at pelting time," says the editor, "will turn the [Friends of Animals] into insane attackers of the industry." [13]

I am told by a professional pelter that he kills mink cleanly and quickly by injecting a nicotine-base insecticide into the heart. Others use denatured alcohol or ether. In the past, mink were killed with cyanide, electrocuted, squeezed in a machine, or struck to dislocate the neck. (When I last killed a fur seal pup for scientific study I injected nicotine into its heart; the pup died in less than thirty seconds.)

⌘

WHAT is the future of the fur-bearing animals of the United States? Let me start on a gloomy note. Americans, growing in numbers and in per capita demand for goods and energy, are yearly destroying over 1 million acres of wildlife habitat. Of the original 127 million acres of wetlands in the United States—the home of the beaver, mink, muskrat, and otter—more than 57 million have been drained for dry-land use. Corporate farming, logging, strip mining, damming for reservoirs, dredging for harbors, gutting of stream channels for quick runoff, laying of pipelines for gas and oil, surfacing of land for cities, highways, and airports—these are the changes in the landscape that threaten the breeding places of the furbearers. Beneath and above the visible damage to the American landscape are the contaminants and pollutants, the biocides whose poisonous effects cause mounting alarm as each is brought to the open and measured.

Nonetheless, I believe that new patterns of thought and action in the conservation of wildlife will, if sustained, assure the future of the fur-bearing species. The Wilderness Act of 1964 established a system of nearly roadless areas, most of them untrapped.[14] Though the giant Forest Service, a diehard advocate of multiple use, has been slow to obey the mandate of the act, the Wilderness System now includes 11 million acres. I perceive a rising trend by the states to acquire land for wildlife use; in Washington, the Game Department is the second largest owner of State land. Notwithstanding that most game departments are locked in on the primary goal of consumptive use, a piece of land in public ownership offers more security for wildlife than one in private hands. The future of the Pribilof Islands as a refuge for seals is debated. The Marine Mammal Protection Act of 1972 opens the way for renegotiation of the fur seal treaty with the goal of getting the United States out of the seal-killing business.

The hazard to fur-bearing animals of poisonous chemicals scattered on public land was sharply reduced in 1972. An executive order banned the use of strychnine, cyanide, sodium fluoracetate (compound 1080), and similar poisons,[15] some of which had been used for more than fifty years in a government war against badgers, bears, bobcats, cougars, coyotes, foxes, and wolves of the western range—not to mention roving pet animals and harmless birds.

A rising market for fake furs, "mink in masquerade," is certain to relieve pressure on wild furbearers. E. F. Timme and Son, a supplier of fabrics, is pushing a line of forty-five "Timme-Tation" furs. In an advertisement in *Vogue,* it questions: "Does the international beauty who recently bought a 10-skin tiger maxi-coat know that there are now only 592 tigers left alive?"[16] Ben Kahn and Georges Kaplan, American furriers, have a novel approach—they are making silkscreen prints on albino ranch-bred mink skins, using the design patterns of real leopard, zebra, cheetah, tiger, and giraffe.[17] (Never underestimate the imagination of a New York furrier.)

The new emphasis on fake furs is unpopular with the director of the fur and leather department of the Amalgamated Meat Cutters and Butchers Union (AFL/CIO). He calls upon the fur industry to attack manufacturers of synthetic fur fibers who "identify a natural fur coat with the brutal slaying of baby seals . . . yet continue to manufacture bombs, gas and napalm." [18] He does not seem to understand that it is well within American mores to produce hospital cotton and guncotton in the same factory.

As I follow the trend in fur fashions away from wild-taken skins toward ranch-bred and fake, I am reminded that American women in my mother's time were asked to shed their plumage to save the egret, goura pigeon, ostrich, and bird of paradise. New York customs agents clipped the feathers from the hats of angry women newly arrived from Paris and London. Tradition had made the wearing of wild feathers seem logical and necessary; a deepening sense of nature—one of the purest of common senses—broke the habit.

I suggest a final reason for optimism toward the future of wild fur-bearing animals: a rising tide of protest against the use of the steel leghold trap. (It was banned in Britain in 1958.) "If you want a rough idea of the leghold trap," writes a member of the Universities Federation for Animal Welfare, "just imagine that the door of your car has been slammed across the fingers of your bare hand. Imagine that the door is jammed shut—and imagine that you are then left with your hand so caught until you either starve to death, or freeze to death—or tear your hand apart." [19]

At the close of 1972, two states, Hawaii and Florida, had banned the leghold trap. A bill is pending in Congress to forbid the traffic in skins of any animal taken by leghold traps in the United States or abroad.[20] The large national mail-order catalogs no longer offer steel traps, though the catalog of a specialty firm "famous since 1848" for its animal traps, lists a wide variety, including a 575-pound dandy for grizzly bear. The Canadian Association for Humane Trapping considers a humane trap to be one that kills almost instantly or renders an animal unconscious until it dies. The Association has exchanged free of charge over $35,000 worth of its own traps (Conibear model) for leghold types.

In search of a distillate of wisdom on the whole business of killing for the fur trade, I turn to a 1972 position paper issued by the International Union for the Conservation of Nature and Natural Resources. The Union, from scientific and biological bases, speaks clearly for the preservation of wildlife populations by the use of every tool in man's technology, while arguing (not inconsistently) for exploitation of the populations at sustainable rates.[21]

I do not reproach the Union; it is staffed by practical people; it is not supposed to pass judgment on moral issues; it is not charged with understanding the attitude of the new conservationists toward the nature that surrounds us all. Nonetheless, I believe that its position vis-à-vis the fur trade will prove in the long run to be wrong, or unacceptable to mankind, which is roughly the same thing.

CHAPTER 5

Killing for Science

IN 1907, a wild-animal collector heard that a few northern elephant seals were still alive on Guadalupe Island, off the west coast of Mexico. He cabled to Baron Rothschild, director of the public museum at Tring, England, and received an order for specimens. He sailed to the island, where he found about forty seals. "My heart smote me," he wrote, "when I thought of killing these wonderful animals with such eyes of liquid velvet." [1] Then he shot fourteen. Those that escaped to the water became the ancestors of a population which has now risen, under protection, to 30,000, and has spread to central California.

Today, the museums and private collections of North America hold the certified remains of about 6 million birds and mammals killed for scientific study.[2] Some bird-and-beast watchers are unsympathetic to the killing of wildlife for research, while, on their part, some museum curators are cool toward bird-and-beast watchers. When T. Gilbert Pearson was struggling to get the young Audubon Association (as it was then called) on its feet, he went to Washington to solicit help from the United States Biological Survey. He was rebuffed. One of the staff "was hostile and said that if the Association did not actually advocate the stopping of scientific collecting it at least was to blame for what was taking place because it was arousing interest over the country in birds, which reacted against collectors." [3] In later years, when a broader conservation ethic began to take shape in America, the Association and the Survey realized that they were both headed in the same direction. The Association learned that understanding of ecological life histories—a basis of wildlife conservation—involves killing some animals, while the Survey learned to listen for sounds of a concern for life in the twittering of the watchers.

An unwritten set of priorities in zoology says that an investigator should depend for material, first on living undisturbed animals in their natural habitat, then on animals in captivity (or immobilized by harmless drugs), then on animals found dead through accident or disease, then on animals (such as deer, seals, and whales) killed in sport or commercial hunting, and finally on animals killed deliberately for scientific study.

By any definition, necrology is not the study of life, though it can expose the machinery of life. Let me try to explain why some individuals must die if man is ever to understand the fullness of life in the whole species of which the individual is a part.

Faced with an unknown fauna in an unexplored country, the zoologist begins to scout and survey, to find out what kinds of animals live there, how they differ from their relatives in adjacent populations, in what ecological crannies they abide, and how widely they wander. He studies their distribution and variation. He may see runways, grass clippings, and toilet piles in a meadow and know that some kind of vole or lemming lives here, but he cannot identify it until he has trapped a few specimens, prepared their skins and skulls for permanent storage, and compared them with others in a museum collection. The so-called red wolf has cropped up in the literature of the American Southwest for three hundred years, but because few specimens were collected when the beast was common, its relationship to the gray wolf and coyote is still a mystery. It may be in the direct line of ancestry of all wolves of America. A mere 100 red wolves remain along the coasts of Texas and Louisiana.

In research on the northern fur seals under a treaty agreement, biologists of North America and Asia kill hundreds of seals every year on the North Pacific Ocean. Some seals are wearing tags which indicate the land of their birth. About one-third of the seals born in Alaska spend their first few winters in waters off Japan, fraternizing there with Soviet seals. This fact of intermingling, learned through the killing of specimens, comes in handy in treaty discussions of national ownership of the seals.

When birds or mammals are suspected of doing damage to agricultural crops, stored foods, tree plantations, or commercial fisheries, some individuals must be killed, and their stomach contents examined to find out what they are feeding on. The first wildlife agency of the United States Government, the Division of Ornithology and Mammalogy, was established in 1896 at the request of farmers annoyed by the attacks of crows and field mice upon their crops.

As an alternative to killing an animal—a deer, for example—the biologist can watch it through binoculars in the act of browsing upon identifiable plants, or he can examine the chewed remains of the plants afterward, or he can examine the droppings (known as "scats"). A researcher in Colorado wanted to know the percentage of different foods eaten by deer on an experimental forest. He raised orphan fawns from wild stock, then turned the tame animals loose in large pens where he could spy on their choice of vegetation.

When I spent the summer of 1937 on a wildlife inventory of the Aleutian Islands I had the dreary job of picking up after blue foxes. Our team objective was to estimate, through scat analysis, whether the foxes on certain islands were feeding mainly on beach organisms (such as sand fleas) or on birds (such as murres, petrels, auklets, gulls, and ptarmigan). Where bird remains were

abundant in the scats, we recommended that the foxes be removed in order to spare the birds. The foxes were exotic; they had been planted in the Aleutians by fur trappers after World War One.

It is often necessary to kill a bird or mammal to be absolutely certain of its food habits and, perhaps equally important, to obtain the kind of firm evidence that will re-educate a public mistaken in its notion of those habits. Biologists found salmon in only 2.4 percent of nearly 10,000 seal stomachs collected in the northeastern Pacific Ocean, thus squelching a widespread belief that fur seals do great damage to salmon. The seals eat, in fact, more than 100 kinds of fishes and squids. In New Hampshire, the food remains in 600 wildcat stomachs showed that the cats were eating, in order of importance, rabbits, deer, squirrels, porcupines, mice, birds, furbearers, and shrews.

One day in my laboratory when I was examining the bodies of young fur seals for research, I discovered that a distinct band is deposited in the ivory of the teeth during each nursing episode, for a total of about a dozen bands during the suckling season. That anatomical fact confirmed a deduction which biologists had made after watching the seals day after day on their nursing grounds. Another technique was later developed: drug-immobilizing wild animals such as polar bears and caribou, pulling a sample tooth from each one, and releasing the drowsy victim to recover.

Killing and dissecting a wild animal cannot be

avoided if one is to probe the mysteries of its reproduction. Ovaries, testes, and embryos give evidence of the pregnancy rate, sexual season, years of sexual life, incidence of twins, sex ratio of fetuses, and other vital data. An enormous fund of information on reproduction has been built upon dissection of birds and mammals killed in sport or for the market.

I received a shock one day when a Western Union operator called me and began, doubtfully, "I think this may be a death message." Pause. "Otaria Byronia died today do you want body?" The wire was from Belle Benchley, director of the San Diego Zoo; one of her sea lions had died and she was inquiring whether I could use the remains for science.

In the tropics, where many birds and mammals carry diseases transmittable to man, thousands of animals are routinely killed every year for study of their disease and parasite loads.

When a wild animal is seen to be ill or emaciated, killing and examining it may give a clue to some environmental imbalance which can be corrected for the benefit of other animals in the population. The disputed question of whether petroleum and pesticides in California waters are responsible for abortion in sea lions will eventually be answered by killing animals at random, measuring the biocide levels in their tissues, and correlating the levels with reproductive condition.

When a biologist kills an animal with intent to use its tissues as a measure of environmental poisoning, he tries to be tactful. He does not shoot a rare California brown pelican simply to measure its load of DDT, though he would be justified in shooting a murre from a colony of thousands for the same end. He kills a few sea lions in an effort to understand a high incidence of abortion among them, though he would not shoot them on Seal Rocks below Cliff House, San Francisco.

A proposal to kill for science caused a flareup between state and federal governments which is still smoldering. When, in 1967, the superintendent of Carlsbad Caverns National Park approved the killing of fifty deer for research, he started a legal fight which was to last for more than two years and move up to the Supreme Court. The fight centered around a question which seems on the surface rather petty but which has important implications—must the federal government obtain a license from a state game department before it can kill animals on its own public land? A local court said yes, it must—the right of the government is no greater than that of an ordinary landowner. A higher court reversed the decision, whereupon the local game commission appealed to the Supreme Court, which declined to enter the controversy.[4] It would seem, then, that the National Park Service does have responsibility for all the natural elements, living as well as scenic, for which its preserves were originally set aside.

The ordinary scientific collector operates under state or federal permits that spell out responsibilities. He can take only certain species in certain numbers, at certain places, and for specific reasons. I should like to see the permit system strengthened by banning all killing for private collections, allowing it only for institutions of science and education. Some of my colleagues disagree, saying that a private collector has more enthusiasm and dedication than a public collector.

Indeed, some valuable collections have been made by men like Walter W. Dalquest, who used his collection as the basis for a book on the mammals of Washington [5] and later turned it over to a university. Many outstanding biologists trace their interest in wildlife from childhood when they began to collect bird eggs and skins, and frogs and toads. Ira Gabrielson, author of seven books, was a born naturalist. He became the first director of the United States Fish and Wildlife Service, and later president of the Wildlife Management Institute. Long into mature life he has continued to "put up" skins for science. Gabrielson and his kind are drawn to the strangeness and beauty of creation, at first by sight and touch of the bird or beast and later by deep intellectual curiosity.

I know that a public collector—a scientist in a museum or college—can be as thoughtless as a private collector. In early June, 1971, a teacher discovered a pair of black-capped gnatcatchers nesting on Sonoita Creek in southeastern Arizona. The birds were perky little things, washed in pale colors of blue and brown, set off with black and white. (The female looked a bit unusual, but more of this in a moment.) The birds represented a

Mexican species that had never before been known to nest in the United States. Word of the find spread quickly via birdwatcher grapevine and on June 19 twenty people were spying on the nest, which now contained three fledglings. Arnold Small, professor of biology at Harbor College, Los Angeles, was there. So was a graduate student in zoology at the University of Arizona. Working together, they captured the parent birds by net and the fledglings by hand, then observed them carefully, taking notes, measurements, and color photographs. They released the birds unharmed.

On June 22, the student, acting on the advice of the curator of birds at the University of Arizona, returned to the nest, killed the five birds, and preserved their skins for study. His aim was to solve a riddle: Was the mother bird a black-capped gnatcatcher or was she a blue-gray gnatcatcher which had mated outside her tribe? This could be settled by comparing her skin, feather by feather, with those of other gnatcatchers in the university cabinets.

Many were angered by the shooting. Some enthusiasts were on their way from California to watch the birds through binoculars. Dr. Small himself protested: "In this day of ecological awareness and of professing reverence for nature and life itself, what right does any individual have to kill a bird of this kind? Does the possession of a valid collecting permit for Arizona give that individual dominion over the birds of that state? If I were issued a 'bird-watching permit' [there is no such] for Arizona would I have equal rights to view that bird alive rather than executed?" [6]

The shoot-out on Sonoita Creek was an unintentional cruelty. It did not fit into the new morality. People now have emotional needs which are not to be satisfied by learning, at the cost of her life, that a female *Polioptila nigriceps* had not, in fact, strayed from the ways of her tribe.

John Fowles, British poet and novelist, believes intensely that no moral choice of our time is clearer than the sparing of life. He passed through an early stage of collecting butterflies, eggs, and plants; moved on to shooting and fishing—"a black period in my relations to nature"—and became a writer. "The deepest thing we can learn about nature," he believes, "is not how it works, but that it is *the poetry of survival*. The greatest reality is that the watcher has survived and the watched survives. It is the timelessness woven through time, the cross-weft of all being that passes. Nobody who has comprehended this can feel alone in nature, can ever feel the absolute hostility of time. However strange the land or the city or the personal situation, some tree, some flower will still knit us into this universe all we brief-lived things co-habit; will mesh us into the great machine. That is why I love nature; because it reconciles me with the imperfections of my own condition, of our whole human condition, of the all that is. My freedom depends totally on its freedom. Without my freedom, I should not want to live." [7]

CHAPTER 6

Sealing: A Threat to the Antarctic?

THE South Pole of earth is central to a mighty continent where a man can still walk unfeared by birds and beasts, a land of silence and whiteness where the temperature drops to 127 degrees below zero and the deepest ice has lain in its bed for 2,000 centuries. This is the Antarctic. Along its coastline of 18,500 miles and among its drifting icebergs live uncounted numbers of seals. One estimate places the total at 30 million, though that high figure is based on extrapolation to many regions where no counts have been made.[1] The crabeater seal is most abundant, representing about 95 percent of the seal populations. Crabeaters live on the floating ice of the Southern Ocean, far from land. They feed on plankton; they exploit organisms at a low level of the marine food-ladder. The Weddell seal (2 percent), leopard seal (2 percent), and Ross seal (1 percent), feed on fishes, squids, or warm-blooded vertebrates. Now and then a fur seal or an elephant seal will wander south to the edge of pack ice, though none will breed there.

The Antarctic continent was discovered in 1820. Most of the subantarctic islands had been discovered earlier—South Georgia first in 1778. In the span of only fifty years, from 1780 to 1830, the fur seals and elephant seals which breed on islands north of the pack ice were nearly wiped out. The four seals of the Antarctic proper have never been hunted commercially—with one minor exception in 1964.

In 1959, the representatives of twelve nations, including the United States, signed a remarkable document, the Antarctic Treaty. They agreed to respect forever the peaceful uses of the land and the ice shelves (but not to alter existing rights on the high seas or sea ice) south of Latitude Sixty South, to press no claims of national sovereignty, to cooperate in research, and to provide for open inspection of one another's scientific stations. In 1964 I was privileged to visit Antarctica on the first American team to exercise that right of inspection. We called at the New Zealand and Soviet bases and flew over the remote French base at Dumont d'Urville. I shall never lose the memory of that land of coldness and purity, nor shall I lose the inner glow that came from giving testimony there for a new kind of international science.

But even as we left Antarctica we learned that commercial sealers were exploring the "no man's water" unprotected by treaty—the pack ice of the high seas. From August to October (southern spring) in 1964, the private Norwegian vessel *Polarhav* worked in the Weddell and Scotia seas of the Southern Ocean. Her crew took 1,127 seals, including 272 near-term fetuses and 3 newborn pups. The voyage was scientifically, though not commercially, profitable. It was a thin wedge that could open the Southern Ocean, already taxed by abusive whaling, to commercial sealing.

Eight years later, representatives of the twelve governments which originally signed the Antarctic Treaty concluded a Convention for the Conservation of Antarctic Seals. It was opened for signature on June 1, 1972, and was signed by all twelve representatives before the end of 1972. The Convention applies to the land, water, and ice south of latitude Sixty South. For crabeater, leopard, and Weddell seals the combined annual catch limit is set at 192,000; Ross seals are protected. The Convention establishes closed seasons, closed areas, and other safeguards which are adequate to preserve all the species.[2] Though the United States delegation made a vigorous attempt to insert provisions for international inspection and enforcement of sealing rules, it was unsuccessful. For moral effect, however, the delegation placed on record its minority view: "There is no known intention in the U.S. of commencing commercial sealing in the Antarctic, and the U.S. Government would prefer that none be initiated." [3]

Sealing: A Threat to the Antarctic?

An official of a large Norwegian sealing company has stated that the company does not know of any Norwegian plans for sealing in Antarctic waters and that because of the distance sealing would probably be too expensive. He emphasized that Norway would observe any international agreements or recommendations.[4]

The Convention says nothing about the salvaging of seal carcasses, though it does provide (in Article 6) for review of sealing operations in the event that sealing does get under way. If Canadian harp sealing is a precedent, only the skins of the Antarctic seals will be saved; the bodies will be left on the ice. Because the maximum weight for crabeater seals is about 500 pounds, and for Weddell and leopard seals, 1,000 pounds, the total waste could be substantial.

World reaction to the news that the pack ice of the Southern Ocean was "opened for sealing" was mixed. The news was in fact incorrect, for the Southern Ocean had always been open for sealing. While the delegates were drawing up the Convention, the National Audubon Society, the New York Zoological Society, and the Defenders of Wildlife issued a joint statement to the Secretary of State. "[We] can find no rational basis for the introduction of commercial sealing into Antarctica. We cannot countenance this destruction of the earth's last remaining ecologically intact continent. We believe it is contrary to the wishes and best interests of a majority of the American people. Should the United States sign a Convention to this effect, we could not support ratifica-

87

tion." [5] The protesting groups were inspired by moral considerations and also by annoyance that the conference was surrounded by a secrecy which kept most American wildlife groups from expressing their concerns on the conference floor. But secrecy was not intended. The U.S. State Department only at the last moment woke up to the strength of public opinion about sealing and realized that it had not consulted widely enough.

Writer Cleveland Amory protested that "the animals of an entire continent were sold out" by the State Department. The *New York Times* declared that "the world cannot afford to lose [by commercial exploitation] a vast untouched observatory." The Second World Conference on National Parks recommended that the Antarctic continent and the surrounding seas be made the first world park, under the auspices of the United Nations.[6]

On the other side of the argument, among those who thought that the sealing convention represented a wise accommodation without sacrifice of principle, was Nigel Sitwell, publisher of *Animals* magazine. "If sealing is to be stopped," he wrote in that journal, "it is likely to be stopped by pressure of public opinion. We can mobilise public opinion whether or not a convention has been signed. Surely it is better to have a set of guiding rules in the meantime, even before sealing is abolished. . . . One must not be afraid of being realistic." [7] Elsewhere he stated: "I am not in favor of commercial sealing, but without a convention there would have been no limit on numbers taken by any nation that wanted to start. And we mustn't forget that these are international waters." [8]

A persuasive opinion came from Brian Roberts, leader of the British delegation to the conference and an old Antarctic hand. In hammering out the articles of the Convention, "we have tried," he said, "to establish enough warning lights to deter any one from investing capital in such an enterprise. . . . Note that this Convention is primarily a deterrent, with provisions for stronger action should this become necessary. The deterrents are rather more vague than I would like, but it has been a long and heavy task, spreading over more than ten years. We need to watch this closely as *the first major experiment in international arrangements for the conservation of a natural resource which is not yet being exploited.* I hope that we may never need to invoke its provisions in the law courts, but I still feel entirely convinced that we should try to secure arrangements of this kind before any specific problems force unsatisfactory compromises." [9]

The Convention clearly represents a world consensus that private industry on the new frontier of the Southern Ocean shall be controlled by one means or another. It is likely to be followed by treaties to regulate commercial fishing, hunting of penguins, and cropping of krill—the planktonic mix of small, free-swimming crustaceans, of which about 50 million tons are produced in the Southern Ocean every year.

Antarctic sealing fits neatly into this book because it exemplifies a clash between the old conservationists, who insist that killing is an essential, primary tool of wildlife management, and the new ones who maintain that killing should always be a secondary resort. For the reasons expressed by Roberts, I approve the 1972 Convention, though I hope that none of the signatory nations will actually begin sealing.

If we will it to be so, Antarctica and her shining mantle will become a refuge for an idea—that man is able to leave at least one place on earth where he and his fellow creatures of the wilderness can move in peace in their separate ways. Man cannot improve the Great White Continent; the question is, will he leave it alone?

CHAPTER 7

Shuffling
Wildlife Faunas

THERE will always be men who are driven, as though by a procreative urge, to "plant" wild animals in foreign places. Eighteenth-century navigators dropped live goats and pigs on oceanic islands to insure a food supply for later visitors. Out of nostalgia, the Natural History Society of British Columbia planted English skylarks near Victoria in 1903; the descendants of those birds are flourishing today. The story of mammal plantings in New Zealand is often used to impress young students of wild-life management. At the time of its discovery by Europeans, the mammal fauna of New Zealand included only two kinds of bats and the Polynesian dog and rat; no animal whatsoever browsed on the green vegetation of those islands. Now thirty-two imported species are firmly fixed in the fauna of New Zealand. Populations of deer and opossums are running out of control, causing damage to crops, livestock, and soil amounting to tens of millions of dollars a year.

As a result of the planting urge, many kinds of exotic big-game animals are roaming nowadays on ranches of Texas and New Mexico. Some are held on shooting preserves, some are held (in cooperation with city zoos) to preserve endangered species, and others are held purely for the pleasure of the ranch owners. The Y.O. Ranch in Texas, covering 75,000 acres, is said to be America's largest shooting ground for exotic game.[1] To a degree, of course, the kind of animals a man chooses to keep on his own place is his own business, and to a degree it is not, even in Texas. History is filled with stories of escaped animals that later became permanent pests—the Russian wild boar, the red fox, gray squirrel, muskrat, nutria, rabbit, mongoose, and, notably, the domestic goat, which has run wild and devasted so many oceanic islands. Time and again, wildlife managers are faced with the zoological warning: You will be wiser to improve the environment of the native species—those that have adapted through centuries of time—than to be dazzled by the presumed advantages of creatures from other lands.

Since 1900, the United States government has kept a record of the live birds and mammals imported into this country. In the year of latest report, 1969, the numbers were astonishing; and that was not an unusual year.

Shuffling Wildlife Faunas

	Individuals	Species
Birds	647,318	more than 800
Mammals	122,991	338

They were imported for zoos and aquariums, for research laboratories, for the pet trade, and for private citizens. Of the birds, 66 percent were finches of one family; they probably went to pet shops. Eighty-nine percent of the mammals were primates; most of them probably went to laboratories.[2] Of all the animals, I suppose that fewer than 1 percent escaped or were turned loose in the wild.

The little gray-breasted monk parakeet, imported by the thousands from South America as a caged bird, has now escaped and has established breeding colonies in New York, North Dakota, Virginia, and Michigan. It is an agricultural pest in its homeland, and when it spreads to the southern states it will surely cause damage to crops. The bird fauna of Florida already includes many foreign species which are the descendants of escaped pets—spotted-breasted oriole, red-whiskered bulbul, canary-winged parakeet, budgerigar, ringed turtledove, Indian ring-necked parrot, orange-chinned parakeet, double yellow-headed parrot, Java sparrow, and African crowned crane. Within a few years, the visitor to Florida, finding himself surrounded by exotic birds, and theme parks, and Disney-type fantasy lands, may be unable to tell the real world from the unreal. (Some, of course, go to such places to blur that distinction.)

In 1973, the delegates of about eighty nations signed

an International Convention on Trade in Endangered Species of Wild Fauna and Flora, which establishes control over the export and import of about 650 species of rare plants and animals.[3] Though the delegates were concerned on this occasion only with threatened species, perhaps a future group will deal with international shuffling of all species.

 ❧

THE greatest push for transplanting animals in the United States comes from hunters. They want either to add target species to the countryside or to restore species which were exterminated in the earlier, more exploitative years of the country's history. The new conservationists are uneasy about the target objective; it suggests the eventuality that the countryside will become an open zoo. They support the restoration of depleted forms of life, especially when the replacements are closely related to those which were exterminated.

Hunters point with pride to the introduction of ring-necked pheasants, brought from Shanghai in 1882 and released near Portland, Oregon. The descendants of those birds, and later importations, have adapted beautifully to America, mainly because pheasants are tolerant of most habitats from sea level to 8,000 feet, and from open prairie to brushland. In South Dakota, hunters killed more than 3 million ringnecks in a single year.

In the northwestern corner of Washington State,

the rugged, snow-covered Olympic Mountains rise to elevations above 7,000 feet. Long ago this area was a glacial island, surrounded by Pleistocene ice on three sides and by the Pacific Ocean on the fourth. As the ice melted, a forest took its place. The mountains were isolated by ice for untold centuries and by a forest for 15,000 years, with the result that certain mammals of the Rocky Mountains, including the wild goat, never reached the island. That mistake of nature was corrected by game commissioners who, in the 1920s and 1930s, obtained goats from Canada and Alaska and released them in the Olympics. By 1973, the goat population had grown to more than 400.

Now botanists can never know the vegetation of a unique, unbrowsed Olympic alpine meadow. Zoologists can study—for what it is worth—a hybrid stock of goats containing the blood of three races. Most hikers will continue to enjoy the sight of goats without knowing, or needing to know, that the animals are alien. Local hunters never did get a shot at the goats, for the Olympic Mountains were made a national park, and the Washington Game Department subsequently gave protection to those goats which wandered outside the boundaries of the park.

Individual game departments among themselves engage in a good deal of wild-animal swapping, while the federal government cooperates by searching in foreign lands for suitable species for introduction. The foreign game investigation program of the Department of the Interior has looked into the possibilities of at least 150 kinds of birds. Among them are francolin, jungle-fowl, tinamou, and many varieties of pheasants, partridges, and grouse.[4]

I believe that the federal program was poorly conceived. It disturbs the native faunas and thereby dilutes the essence of America. We who go to the country for recreation are captive onlookers, so to speak, at exotic animals turned loose, not in a beast park which we could visit or not by choice, but on the public commons.

The Department of the Interior has a prepared answer to my kind of complaint. "Many parts of our country," it says, "have changed irreversibly as a result of human population movement and consequent agriculture and industry. In these, resident native species have become extirpated because they were intolerant of habitat changes. The foreign introduction program takes cognizance of this and seeks to bring species that can exist in such areas, succeed and become established."[5]

The point, however, is not whether exotics can be established but whether they ought to be.

Beyond the wealthy suburbs of Pennsylvania cities, socialites who formerly rode to hounds after foxes have accepted miniaturization—they now ride to beagles after rabbits. They chase the local cottontails, and they chase jack rabbits, imported from Kansas in lots of up to ten dozen. Though it is unlikely that a plains jack rabbit would survive and reproduce in the East, the dumping of rabbits anywhere outside their native range is fraught with danger and ought to be forbidden. I have seen the awful damage done by rabbits released years ago on the San Juan Islands of Washington.

Of all the reasons for planting wildlife, that of providing penned-in targets is perhaps the least defensible. Three brothers in Monroe County, Wisconsin, recently proposed to operate a shooting ground where European boars, Japanese deer, Spanish rams and goats, and black bears (all male trophy animals) would be held within a 500-acre plot. For a fee, men armed with rifles, handguns, or bows and arrows would be allowed to "hunt" these animals. The local game manager for the Department of Natural Resources stated: "Conservation wardens are very much interested in this project. It's the first in the state and I can foresee no problems of any kind." [6] No problems? The unfortunate manager had not learned in school that wildlife management is undertaken first for the good of people and second for the good of wildlife. The people of Monroe County raised an immediate outcry in newspapers and in public hearings. At last report, the brothers had been denied permission to proceed with their plan.

Scanning a national directory of shooting preserves, I saw the name Safari Island, in Puget Sound. I wrote for a brochure from the contact agent. I was answered by a cautious telephone call, and when I said that I was a writer, I heard no more from the agent. In a roundabout way I got the brochure and other advertisements. I learned that "Safari Island" is beautiful Spieden Island, bought and renamed in 1969 by a corporation which has stocked it with quail, Chinese pheasant, guinea fowl, chukkar partridge, jungle fowl, turkey, African Barbary sheep, Indian black buck, Corsican mouflon sheep, Spanish goat, Indian spotted deer, Japanese sika deer, hybrid four-horned sheep, and European fallow deer. "Let's go to the hunter's paradise on Safari Island," says one of the ads. For only $590, one can have "two full days and nights with deluxe catering and experienced guide," and shoot one mouflon ram and one Spanish goat [7]—tame stock released on an island from which they cannot hope to escape.

I am offended by the type of hunting offered in this brochure, and I feel sorry for the visitors whose education has left them so lacking in grasp of earthly values—so insensitive to the color and beauty and music of natural arrangements. It is a pity that visitors—unaware of these free values—will pay to shoot goats in a barnyard.

A FEW wild animals have been introduced as furbearers or as food for furbearers. The Arctic fox was stocked on many oceanic islands in Canada and Alaska after World War One when fur prices rose dramatically. The tundra squirrel and varying hare were planted on some of the same islands as food for the foxes.

I helped my father trap hares alive in the Puget Sound lowlands in the 1920s for shipment to Alaska, and I am one of the few sane men who have tried to plant

mice. In 1940 I tried without success to translocate lemming mice from St. George Island to St. Paul Island,
Alaska. I was unsuccessful, probably because I took stock
from a swarming overpopulation which—according to
latest theory—would have carried a hidden genetic
factor for its own decline.

The transplanting of wild animals as food for native
peoples has potential value, though the only two examples I know of were not entirely successful. Reindeer
(semiwild caribou) were planted on the Pribilof Islands
in 1911. On one island, the stock fizzled out after forty
years for unknown reasons. On the other, it survived for
fifteen years, suddenly erupted into more than 2,000 animals, then died out more quickly than it had grown.
Thirty-four musk-oxen were planted in 1930 on Nunivak
Island in the Bering Sea, 700 miles from the historic
rangeland of the species along the Arctic Slope. (Hunters had exterminated them there in the 1850s.) The
Nunivak herd has swelled to about 700 animals and
sportsmen are calling for a hunt. As of 1973, the federal
government had not agreed to open a sport-hunting
season, although it was under pressure to do so.

NONE of my criticisms of transplanting are directed at restoring species to their former haunts, an operation which
has wide public support. The graceful sea otter, exterminated fifty years ago from most of the Pacific coast
south of the Alaska Peninsula, has been restored in token

numbers to the shores of southeast Alaska, British Columbia, Washington, and Oregon.

For students of wildlife research, the effort to find methods of capturing and transporting sea otters is a classic example. The first experiment was launched in 1951. Thirty-five otters were netted; all died before they could be placed aboard a waiting ship. Fifteen years were to pass before biologists identified a peculiar and critical need of the otters—their silky fur must be kept absolutely clean. More than a hundred otters lost their lives in nets and in holding pens, on ships and aircraft, before that need became obvious. The otter spends half of its waking hours in grooming and preening. When confined to a pen that seems, to human eyes, reasonably clean, an otter may die within a few days.[8]

The Oregon Game Commission deserves credit for restoring bighorn sheep to the Wallowa Mountains where the last native animals were exterminated around 1940. Forty sheep, from stock trapped in the Canadian Rockies, were released in Oregon in 1972. The bighorn, chosen by the United States Postal Service as a symbolic figure for its 1972 Wildlife Conservation Stamp, is truly endangered. Biologists give it a fighting chance, though they are not sure how to save the kind of wilderness which the animal needs for survival.

☙

THE new conservationists are skeptical of any proposal to transplant an animal until research has shown that the transfer will fill an ecological void. The Province of New-foundland is cautiously introducing certain native species —moose, grouse, bison, caribou, and shrew (the last to combat forest insects). It has rejected proposals to import white-tailed deer. Since 1963 it has been studying the impact of squirrels on the vegetation of offshore islands before deciding whether to move them to New-foundland proper. The factors which the government weighs before introducing an animal are: What will the animal mean to Newfoundlanders in increased pleasure and money? Will it bring in new animal diseases? Will it adversely affect any native species, and, conversely, will it benefit existing species? Will it probably survive and multiply? [9] These are the questions that all game managers should ask before shuffling the wildlife faunas.

The urge to transplant animals is rooted in a commendable desire to make one's homeland richer, more varied, and more interesting. Unfortunately, it also stems from a restless reaching out for the exotic, elaborate, and redundant, the new for the sake of newness. The more one learns of the wondrous complexity of the tiniest fraction of native wildlife in its native home, the more accepting one becomes of patterns as they are. The new conservationists call for wider public understanding of the consequences of moving birds and mammals about. Tampering with wildlife, they insist, is surgery on the public body. The public ought to examine the credentials of the surgeons and ask them what they have in mind.

 CHAPTER 8

Getting Along with Wildlife

TWENTY-EIGHT hundred kinds of birds and mammals inhabit North America. Each has its own characteristic behavior, breeding rate, mortality rate, and population cycle. At one time or another, the life style of certain of these animals may become annoying, competitive, harmful, or downright dangerous to man. The human problem of getting along with wild animals increases proportionately as man engineers the surface of the earth, lives more unnaturally, and grows more contemptuous of the wild systems which have supported him during his evolution.

Some members of the Audubon Society will be surprised to learn that in the 1920s the Society condoned the killing of 25,000 minks, raccoons, and muskrats every year on its Rainey Sanctuary in Louisiana in order to furnish some relief to the birds that visited there. In the same period, Jack Miner, the "Birdman of Canada," told of shooting or steel-trapping scores of hawks and weasels as "enemies" of the waterfowl he was befriending.[1] He aligned himself against all flesh eaters as grimly as would a Presbyterian against original sin. I suppose we all tend to take the side of Peter Rabbit against Wily Weasel—but why?

The damage done by wildlife to American property is very great. Crop losses attributable to birds alone are estimated at $50 million to $100 million a year.[2] After the Wildlife Society appointed a committee to study economic losses caused by vertebrates, one of its first recommendations was that "physical losses should be expressed in terms of yield [for example, tons of alfalfa] or quality rather than merely monetary loss."[3] There is indeed little point in trying to estimate the total impact of wildlife upon man's neat arrangements; there is more purpose in looking at individual instances of harm and trying to estimate the social costs, as well as the monetary costs, of minimizing future harm.

≥

THE damage created by North American wildlife can be classed in three groups according to the value damaged —plants, animals, or human life. I choose this classification because it implies that harm is more in the eyes of the harmed than in the mind of the harmer; harm is not the expression of a mean or vicious animality, as some varmint hunters would have us believe.

Farm crops, forest trees, and ornamental vegetation are damaged by gophers, field mice, ground squirrels, jack rabbits and cottontail rabbits, raccoons, blackbirds, grackles, cowbirds, starlings, finches, sparrows, and even game pheasants, quail, and waterfowl. A tree which, in the seed or seedling stage, escapes the teeth of a small mammal may eventually be destroyed by a deer, elk, porcupine, beaver, or black bear.

Few city dwellers realize the abundance of North American birds and mammals. At its peak near the end of summer, the land-bird population north of Mexico is around 20 billion, or nearly a hundred birds for every person.[4] The red-winged blackbird, through its adaptability, is perhaps the most abundant, followed by the crow, starling, and grackle. I have seen a photograph showing 20,000 snow geese on one California rice field.

No one, to my knowledge, has ventured to estimate the number of mammals in North America. The deer mouse (*Peromyscus*), which ranges from salt marshes, deserts, lava fields, and forests to timberline and the edge of Arctic tundra, may be the most abundant native mammal. A runner-up would be the field mouse (*Microtus*). (I wish there were fewer field mice; they girdled the young maples in my yard last winter.)

For several years in the 1950s I worked from a base at Colorado State University on wildlife problems of forest and grazing lands. Damage by the pocket gopher came often into our discussions with livestock ranchers. Rodent-control teams at the time were poisoning the gophers with thallium, strychnine, compound 1080, and warfarin. One team invented a special tractor-driven "burrow builder" which could drop poison on 60 acres a day. On top of Grand Mesa, on a magnificent subalpine meadow at a 10,000-foot elevation, the Forest Service poured herbicide from an airplane to encourage the growth of grass (cattle food) over broad-leaved plants (gopher food). The chemical also killed the scattered aspen, spruce, and streambank willow.

When I left Colorado, I left with a feeling—which could not be defended with statistics—that on most rangelands the gopher is not a bad guy but in fact does good by improving the tilth of the soil, manuring it, and making it more permeable to rainfall. I suspected also that the "knock-'em-dead" approach of control agents, year after year, and one gopher generation after another, is a waste of energy. The rancher would be better off were he to correct land misuses, particularly overgrazing, and learn to accept the gophers along with the complex of predators—hawks, owls, weasels, coyotes, badgers, and bobcats—which for untold centuries have dampened the oscillations of gopher populations.

The valuable evergreen forests of western Washington suffer damage from a surprising source—the black bear. In spring and early summer, when the bears are hard-pressed for food, they strip the outer bark and eat the sapwood of Douglas fir. Though all bears eat a certain amount of bark, those individuals that live on tree farms—vast monocultures—are forced into unusual or exaggerated feeding habits. The typical managed forest is protected artificially from fire and insects; it lacks variety of open spaces and variety of plants and animals, and hence it lacks variety of bear foods. To offset bear damage, the forest owners hire professional trappers and encourage sport-hunting. More than 3,000 bears were killed in western Washington in 1972. An anti-bear cult, supported by a yearly festival, brings visitors to the lumber town of McLeary. Along in midsummer, thousands of men and women gather here to cuss bears and eat bear stew—several hundred gallons of the stuff.

In Rocky Mountain National Park there is a grove of aspen trunks that once were shining white but now are scarred and blackened by the teeth of elk. Mainly because man pre-empted their lowland feeding grounds in winter, the elk were obliged to turn to submarginal foods. Worse than the damage by elk to bark, as in this instance, is complete destruction of young trees, and even worse is destruction of the undergrowth, followed by irreversible loss of the soil.

In the second class of damage by wildlife is harm to animal resources—livestock, game animals, fish, and shellfish. The feeding habits of the flesh eaters—the predatory mammals and raptorial birds—are often competitive with man. Man retaliates. The sad historical fact is that in couterattacking he often chooses the direct, military weapons of gun, booby trap, and poison, and in so doing arouses the resentment of millions who question the morality, the cost-effectiveness, and even the verbal style of his operation.[5]

By style I mean his use of clichés and euphemisms. Predator "control" (that is, killing) is carried on by the federal Branch of Wildlife Services [*sic*] against "probable or known offenders," which, if not offenders, are at least "surplus." A brochure explaining the work of the Branch is entitled *Sharing the Environment*.[6] Though the word "alleviation" may not bother the average reader, it annoys some new conservationists who see a parallel with the word "pacification"—both mean special forms of destruction. Since "predator control" is now fixed in the language of wildlife management, however, I shall continue to use the term.

In the ten-year period 1961–1970, the federal government "removed" 1,016,453 carnivores, in addition to those which died in secret and were unaccounted for. The principal victims were coyotes, followed by bobcats, bears, red wolves, cougars, and gray wolves. No red wolves were killed after 1965, when the government made an about-face and placed the species on its endangered list.[7] In 1972, the government called for a moratorium on the killing of eastern gray wolves, and none too soon, for only 500 to 1,000 were left.

The basic objections to predator control as it has been practiced are that it has caused the decline of wildlife species, such as the wolf; that it is based on exaggerated claims of damage from ranchers and sportsmen; that its use of poison is inhumane, as well as hazardous to non-target animals; and that it is ineffective. What the government calls "prophylactic" poisoning, or preventive poisoning aimed at holding predator populations forever at low levels, simply encourages more vigorous reproduction among the survivors.

In its official policy statement, the government says: "The reduction or suppression of animal numbers should be undertaken only as a means of accomplishing specific management objectives like helping to preserve public health and safety; lessening damage to agricultural production; protecting forest, range, and wildlife resources; and reducing adverse effects of rodents, bats, and birds in urban and industrial areas." [8]

However, these are not specific but general goals. New conservationists have no quarrel with the goals; their protest is against the methods used to reach them. They say that special-interest groups, especially sheepmen and sportsmen, have kept the federal control program alive without regard to a wider public interest. As a kind of environmental degradation in its own way, predator control is as offensive as are strip mining, oil drilling on the continental shelf, and the construction of nuclear reactors in regions of great beauty.

Bureaucratic hostility against predatory animals has at times reminded me of an animal behaviorism known loosely as the urge to kill. A fox, finding itself in a gull colony, may kill and waste more birds than it needs, as

though some stage in its instinctive machinery had mis-
fired.

Though I criticize the federal system of predator
control, I applaud those in government who are trying to
improve it. The Department of Interior has twice called
for advice from biologists and conservationists, first from
the Leopold Committee of 1964 and again from the Cain
Committee of 1971.[9] Moved to action by the latter's report, President Nixon in 1972 banned the use of certain
poisons for killing predatory animals on federal lands.[10]
Shortly thereafter, the Environmental Protection Agency,
by prohibiting interstate shipment of certain systemic
poisons, blocked their use on private lands.

Though the presidential order changed a policy that,
incredibly, had stood unaltered for half a century, further
changes are needed. The order does not ban shooting,
trapping, or denning (digging out the young) of predators, or the use of such poisons as strychnine, zinc phos-
phide, avitrol, starlicide, and certain burrow fumigants
and suffocating cartridges which are employed to kill rodents or birds, and it does permit, subject to the approval
of the heads of certain federal agencies, the use of predator poisons in "emergency" situations.

Some conservationists believe that the federal government, in reducing its effort in predator control, is
merely encouraging the states to carry on programs less
restrained and more offensive than its own. They fear that
the states will resort to two especially inhumane methods,
hunting by greyhounds and shooting from aircraft.

Several states have already begun issuing permits to private landowners to kill predators from planes.

I am encouraged to see the growth of research on predator-prey relationships. The Department of Interior budgeted $300,000 for such research in 1973, as against $110,000 in the previous year. In the past, tens of millions of dollars have been spent to control predators, while the cry "Wolf! Wolf!" resounded from the western hills. If all control had been withdrawn from substantial regions, and the biological effects thereof studied for, say, twenty-year periods, I believe that the resulting biological evidence would have saved millions of dollars. It is useless to look back, but the future is open.

In the third class of damage by wildlife is physical attack upon man. Roger Caras, in an exciting book on animals dangerous to man, concludes that the list of potentially harmful species is endless, yet "if you had the time and energy you could walk completely around the world in any latitude you might select . . . and never fall victim to more than the occasional insect bite." [11]

The only North American wild mammals known to have killed human beings in unprovoked attack are the grizzly bear, black bear, polar bear, and cougar. (No birds have done so.) From the time, 200 years ago, when sizable packs of gray wolves roamed over North America, wolves have inspired great fear, yet no human is known to have been killed by a wolf in North America. There is one possible instance—a man's skeleton, a rusted pistol, and three wolf skeletons dating from some time after the middle 1930s, were found in Alaska.

Public opinion with respect to the graceful big cats known as cougars, mountain lions, or panthers is divided. Cougars are protected by law in about half the states. Texas and South Dakota were still paying bounties for them in 1970, though they no longer do so. I recall the shock of learning, in 1924, that a thirteen-year-old boy living in eastern Washington, had been jumped and killed by a cougar. A posse formed to hunt it eventually killed an emaciated and starving old female cat in whose stomach were remains of human hair and clothing.

Black bears and polar bears have killed humans. Black bears pose a special problem; they are unpredictable. Though they are usually shy and inoffensive, individuals may turn violent without warning. I am told by a zoo keeper that even a tame bear, docile and long familiar with its handler, may attack him without provocation. In the summer of 1971, in Colorado, a 300-pound black bear entered a man's tent in the night, killed him, and dragged his body 50 yards. What dark thoughts did the beast entertain?

Of all the fearsome animals in North America, the grizzly is foremost in the public mind. The grizzly in Alaska—known there as the big brown bear—has always been respected. My colleagues in biology who work in brown-bear country go armed and travel with a companion. The State of Alaska suggests that anyone who goes out to photograph brown bears be accompanied by a competent back-up man with a rifle.

The grizzly has been in the news in recent years as a result of three "meaningless" attacks, all fatal, in national parks. On August 14, 1967, in Glacier National Park, two teen-age girls were killed in their sleeping bags by grizzlies. One was killed at midnight; the other was killed four hours later and 20 miles away by a different bear. On June 25, 1972, a man was attacked by a grizzly in Yellowstone, killed, and partly eaten. The most recent previous bear fatalities in Yellowstone were in 1907, when a visitor chased a cub up a tree, prodded it with an umbrella, and was killed by its mother, and in 1916, when a park employee tried to chase a big grizzly out of a food wagon, and was also killed.

Though only one person in millions is physically harmed by bears in national parks, every attack is magnified in the public mind to a Grimms' fairy tale of horror. The Park Service issues to visitors a brochure filled with advice which, though based on doubtful zoology, is the best that science can offer. Women are advised to stay out of bear country during their menstrual periods, and to abstain from using perfumes, hair spray, deodorants, and cosmetics. "There is some evidence that bears have been attracted by these scents." If attacked, the visitor is advised to play dead. "Lying still under the jaws of a biting bear takes a lot of courage, but it may prevent greater injury or death," maintains the government.[12]

Some of the bears that harm people are truly wild

ones, especially mothers with cubs. Others are camp-ground bums that have been spoiled by easy access to garbage or by handouts of food. When two dumps were abruptly closed in Yellowstone, park rangers were forced to kill twenty-eight grizzlies and fifty-four black bears at nearby campgrounds the following year. The Park Service is now turning to a pack-in, pack-out policy for hikers—which means that they can leave no food scraps. The service is also imposing stiff penalties for feeding bears and is replacing open garbage dumps with incinerators surrounded by bear-proof fencing.

These are straightforward environmental controls. Equally important will be education of the public in the subtle idea that a grizzly bear is a part of wilderness; that a grizzly in a campground is not a real grizzly. The visitor should not expect to see a grizzly. If he does, he is the fortunate person among thousands; if he is attacked, he is the unfortunate one among millions.

AN important, though little-known, kind of damage created by North American wildlife is disease which animals carry to man and to his pets and livestock. Some disease organisms (pathogens) are transmitted by a shuttle agent—a mosquito, bug, louse, flea, tick, or mite —which carries the organism from the blood of one animal to the blood of another. Other pathogens are transmitted by direct bite, by body contact, on food, or on dust particles breathed by the victim. Rabies is perhaps spread by the mist of bat urine in caves.

Disease among wild animals is a normal, common relationship between a large, many-celled host and a smaller organism, a pathogen that lives within its tissues. Each one of the pair has evolved in the presence of the other and each, as attested by its existence today, is biologically successful. Man easily disturbs that relationship. By airplane, he moves in a day from Africa to North America, carrying live germs to a region where the potential host animals have no native resistance. He domesticates sheep, oxen, hogs, cats, dogs, and fowl, then allows them to contact and infect—or be infected by—their relatives in the wild. He pollutes or physically damages wildlife habitats and thereby weakens the vigor of the wildlife species and increases their susceptibility to disease.

According to the United Nations Food and Agricultural Organization, more than 100 diseases are common to both animals and man.[13] If one counts all the strains and varieties, the total may reach 1,000. In the United States during the past twenty years, about 150 persons died of rabies, two of them from simply visiting a cave occupied by rabid bats. In 1971, over 4,000 rabies cases were confirmed from the forty-eight conterminous United States.

When foot-and-mouth disease, a scourge to hoofed animals though not to humans, broke out in California in 1924, drastic measures were taken to contain it. During the next eighteen months, hunters and hired gunmen killed 34,000 deer in nearby Stanislaus National Forest. Ten percent of the deer showed symptoms of the disease.

The plaguelike, often fatal disease known as tularemia (from Tulare County, California) attacks many kinds of wildlife, especially rabbits and rodents. Ninety percent of human cases of tularemia in the United States result from contact with infected cottontail rabbits. It is unlikely that tularemia will ever be eradicated from its myriad pockets of infection in the northern hemisphere.

In the summer of 1959, bubonic plague wiped out all the prairie dogs in an isolated prairie or "park" in Colorado, and a biologist who was studying the disease was himself infected and had to be hospitalized. In another Colorado park, the plague raged from 1964 to 1966, leaving only a few prairie dogs alive.

Brucellosis, which causes abortion in cattle and undulant fever in people, is chronic in bison, moose, and elk in several of the national parks of Canada and the United States. It arouses the anger of cattle ranchers around Yellowstone National Park, who claim that the pathogen, known for many years to be endemic in the park bison, threatens their livestock. They wish that the park rangers would round up the bison, examine them, and destroy infected individuals. But park biologist Mary Meagher says that the possibility of cross infection between bison and cattle is remote—nothing to worry about. Evidently the bison themselves have developed immunity to the bacterium which causes brucellosis, for though it appears in their blood, it does not cause disease or abortion.[14]

The dread disease anthrax is recorded from bison in Canadian national parks. Because the spores of the pathogen persist for a century in soil, bison can be protected only by vaccinating them against the disease.

Among the more loathsome parasitic worms that infect both wildlife and man are the trichina worm, known to live in almost all kinds of mammals, and a dog tapeworm, known to live in carnivores, with a larval stage in rodents. Trichinosis is a painful disease; it persists throughout the life of the victim as millions of larvae embedded in the muscles. It is reported from Eskimos who eat the raw flesh of infected seals and polar bears. In 1970, a mile from the garbage dump of Wallace, Idaho, hunters bagged a young black bear. They made a mild "jerky" of the flesh; it still contained live trichina worms and seriously infected twelve persons who ate it. That case recalls the fatal trans-Arctic balloon flight in 1897 of the Swedish engineer Salomon August Andrée and two companions. Diaries found beside the bodies of the men in 1930 describe the painful symptoms they felt; mummified polar-bear meat found in their last camp contained evidence of trichina worms.

A dog tapeworm causes the painful and sometimes fatal ailment known in man as hydatid disease. The eggs of the worm get into the human alimentary tract in water or food or from unclean fingers. According to the United Nations, hundreds of thousands of persons over the world are infected.[15] In Alaskan villages, house cats and tame foxes carry the worm and are potential carriers of human infection.

Protection of people against the diseases which they suffer in common with wildlife poses many problems for future biologists, veterinarians, and physicians. Pathogens and parasites are not stopped by fences; they move in water and wind and are carried by bird and insects. There is general agreement that the life histories of the pathogens and their animal carriers must be studied in depth; that the lines of transmission of disease must be broken wherever possible, as by inspection and regulation of bird and mammal shipments and by control of wandering house pets; and that the level of public resistance must be raised by providing better food and cleaner surroundings for all.

These solutions make sense to conservationists, who likewise plead for a total ecosystem approach to solutions. They feel intuitively—without claiming special knowledge or offering specific plans—that the future struggle against wildlife diseases will surely involve "natural" treatment of the environments of the pathogens and their carriers.

CHAPTER 9

Bird-and-Beast Watching

In England, a man seen hiding in a wood with his eyes fixed on the distance might be watching a nightingale or a willow warbler; in Africa, he would be hunting for food; in the United States, he would be arrested for trespassing. Making overt love to Nature in the United States is not respectable. I remember the day when, armed with a camera and telephoto lens, I was stalking a pair of cattle egrets. A small boy came sidling up. "You a detectif?" he inquired. We Americans can not easily shake off a Puritan conviction that to be respectable a man must be working at something useful. We have not attained the maturity of the cinematographer Jean Renoir, who holds that all great civilizations have been based on loitering.[1]

Bird-and-Beast Watching

But the leaders of the new conservation movement
say that bird-and-beast watching is an activity deeply
rooted in human culture, nothing new and nothing to be
ashamed of. They emphasize the recreational, educational, scientific, and artistic values contained in the
wildlife resource. They say that bird-and-beast watching
yields a harvest of inspiration.

Their point of view resembles that of Black Elk,
born of the Sioux tribe around 1850, as he tells the
story of his people.

"It is the story of all life that is holy and good to tell,
and of the two-leggeds sharing it with the four-leggeds
and the wings of the air and all green things; for these
are children of one mother and their father is one
Spirit." [2]

In Texas, a new sign along a highway calls attention
to PRAIRIE DOG TOWN, and a million visitors a year
stop to look at the little people of the plains, symbols of
the old frontier. When the Bureau of the Census made its
tally in 1970 it questioned about 9,000 persons twelve
years old and older about their outdoor interests. The
answers indicate that this country supports 6.8 million
"birdwatchers" and 4.5 million "bird and wildlife photog-
raphers," while 26.9 million take "nature walks." [3] I am
not sure what these figures mean, though they do prove
that bird-and-beast watching is important. The managers
of the great National Wildlife Refuge System reported in
1970 the attendance of 12 million visitors presumed to be
"wildlife-oriented." They included sightseers, photog-

raphers, and visitors to nature trails and museums; one in twenty came to hunt.[4] Because few amateur naturalists are members of organized clubs, their total numbers are not easily estimated. A small study made in Canada suggests that fewer than 2 percent are "organized." [5]

ॐ

ONE of the clearest indications that appreciative use of wildlife is gaining popularity is the new attention given by state game departments to non-game programs. I should say renewed attention, for the first American Game Policy, written over forty years ago by Aldo Leopold and others, said plainly that Americans ought to "recognize the nonshooting protectionist and the scientist as sharing with the sportsman and landowners the responsibility for wildlife conservation and to insist on a joint conservation program, jointly formulated and jointly financed." [6]

Down the years, however, the destiny of the people's wildlife has gradually come more and more under control of the game departments, and because these are heavily financed by hunters and trappers, the voices of hunters and trappers now resound in legislative committee halls above the voices of bird-and-beast watchers. Sportsmen talk as though they believe that deer and grouse are special creations—game organisms distinguishable from other kinds of wildlife.

The powerful International Association of Game,

Bird-and-Beast Watching

Fish and Conservation Commissioners established in 1969 a non-game wildlife committee to consider the requirements and potentials of a fauna which, in its opinion, "should be defined by exclusion." [7] That is, "non-game" should describe the wildlife residue left when the useful species have been provided for. Immediately the values of those forms, such as kingfishers and herons, which are customarily appreciated without being killed, are subordinated to the values of those which are hunted for sport or trapped for their skins.

Nathaniel P. Reed, Assistant Secretary of the Interior for Fish and Wildlife and Parks, said in 1971: "I doubt that 10 years ago many of us here would have predicted the tremendous interest in and concern for fish and wildlife so apparent today across the face of our land—not just those species we hunt and fish, but *all* species. It is apparent that not enough has been done or is being done to satisfy the public's interest in the non-game species and non-hunting aspects of game species. Some recreation specialists predict that interest in this type of outdoor recreation will in the future exceed the demand for consumptive uses of these resources, if indeed it hasn't already done so." [8]

The State of Washington is pushing for an expanded non-game wildlife program but, like most of the other states, it does not know where the funding will come from. For a little while yet, it can borrow manpower from its traditional game-oriented branches, but only while the license-paying sportsmen of the state are compliant. The initial cost of a non-game program is estimated at $125,000 a year. The Washington legislature was asked, early in 1973, to approve the sales of a voluntary $30 personalized car license plate, so that birdwatchers could help the wildlife program without having to buy a game license to kill. The bill passed both houses but was vetoed by the governor on the grounds that while the objective was good the scheme, involving earmarked funds, was bad. (As this book goes to press, however, the bill has been enacted via the referendum route by a wide majority. Its popularity rests in part on the fact that it calls for no new taxes.)

Earlier, the Washington legislature had placed the killer whales of Puget Sound under management, thereby legally recognizing non-game animals which excite the admiration of hundreds of thousands of boaters and beachwalkers in the sheltered waters of the state. Pressure for legislation was brought by citizens outraged at the netting of 192 whales between 1965 and 1972. Within the narrow limits of its legal powers, the state is gradually placing other species, such as the harbor seal, chipmunk, and woodchuck, on its protected list. When I learned in 1970 that the white-tailed jack rabbit had been placed on the state's rare and endangered roster I was struck by the profound change in public sympathy toward a creature which, in my younger days, was rounded up in enormous "rabbit drives" and beaten to death by men and boys.

The State of Missouri has called for greater emphasis

on "total ecologic, recreational and educational values [of wildlife] and not principally hunting and fishing. . . . It is essential that a plan of finances be devised that will augment present license fees with revenues from more general sources." [9] "Perhaps," writes a poet in the Conservation Department, "we can buy a ticket back to softer pastimes—the chuckle of a brook or the flute-like call of a wood thrush." [10] A citizen committee in Missouri worked hard for a constitutional amendment which would impose a 1-cent tax on all bottled soft drinks, thereby raising $15 million a year for wildlife conservation, but in late 1972 its petition was knocked out by a legal technicality, thanks to strong lobbying efforts by the bottling industry. The committee intends to try again.

Any lingering doubt that birdwatcher power is real and growing is erased when one learns that Winchester-Western Division of Olin Corporation published in 1972 a booklet on model legislation for a state non-game wildlife conservation program. The booklet is endorsed by the International Association of Game, Fish and Conservation Commissioners and by the Wildlife Society. "To anyone who loves nature in its completeness," says the booklet, "it would be a dreary world with no wildlife but game species; no eagles, ospreys or hawks, no gulls or pelicans; no bobolinks, warblers, prairie dogs, kit foxes, coyotes, grebes, bitterns or flying squirrels." [11] I would add herons, egrets, owls, woodpeckers and flickers, nighthawks, and virtually all small native mammals.

In this model law, non-game species are those "not

123

otherwise legally classified." They are to be managed in the full sense of the word. The costs of the program are to be borne by the general fund of the state and to be "equal in amount to [blank] per centum of the revenues . . . from the sale of hunting, fishing, and trapping licenses, but not less than [blank] dollars." [12]

The Winchester-Western proposal is good, though its curious provision for funding is not. Why should the welfare of the flying squirrel rise and fall with revenues from hunting licenses? Should it not be coupled with a broader public interest?

Hunters and wildlife managers automatically oppose the support of wildlife by general funds. "The fate of wildlife should not rest in the hands of political vagary," is the way it is put by a leading sportsman.[13] But education, welfare, and many other state programs are financed from general taxes; why not wildlife conservation? The posture of many a game department resembles that of highway departments supported by earmarked taxes; both structures tend to become self-perpetuating and irresponsible, selfish and undemocratic. The new conservationists, inside and outside of game departments, say that exclusive hunter support of the people's wildlife is an arrangement whose time is past.

प्र

THE motives of the bird-and-beast watcher are recreational, or a desire for change and renewal; educational, or a desire for a richer life for oneself and others; scientific, or an urge to swell the fund of human knowledge; and artistic, or an urge to experiment and adventure in the pure domain of the aesthetic.

Of all the motives, the educational is perhaps the most central today, for in the process of learning about wildlife people begin to think about ecology, the wasting of natural resources, vanishing species, the proper uses of wild environments, and ultimately the conservation of man himself. When a birdwatcher can stand on Hawk Mountain Sanctuary, Pennsylvania, and in one day count 11,392 broad-winged hawks, he is on the way to respecting the place of raptorial birds in man's economy. When a beastwatcher can see lemmings crowding to their end in Alaska he can, with intellectual profit, wonder about the suicide of overliving and about the social maladjustments of his city friends. If you believe that one of the purposes of education is to show the richness of existence, studying the life styles of wild animals can enhance your recognition of man's closeness in body and spirit to those creatures.

Along the way to self-education in wildlife, the bird-or-beast watcher is sure to be rewarded with the joy of discovery, at which point he may be hooked for life on nature or even turn into a biologist. (This is not a recommendation.) Gilbert White, who wrote the immortal *Natural History of Selborne*,[14] was caught up in the mystery of countryside life. He asked: Where do the swallows go in winter? And why do sparrows dust themselves? He eventually became a nature detective and a nature reporter, slipping easily from the role of amateur to that of professional, or what amounted to professional in his day.

The study of wildlife gives insight into human origins and it helps to explain civilized behavior. We need all possible evidence from the outer world to help us solve— for example—our self-created problems in communication. Biologists try to imitate the pantomime of chimpanzees and the ritual dance of the courting grebe. They measure the power of odoriferous chemicals, or scent, deposited by animals as a sign of their passing. They listen to the sonar voices of dolphins and bats, the bugling of elk, the howling of wolves, and the calling of birds. The mother penguin knows the piping of her own chick, while the baby murre, even before it is hatched, begins to learn the voices of its parents.

Certain biologists specialize in the study of animal populations. (Should they be called theriographers?) They look at the ways in which birds and mammals regulate their own populations. They study territorial needs and limits, and aggressive behavior. What change in his narrow world makes a bison switch from fighting to breeding? Medical biologists look at the therapeutic value of affection, and the manifold ways in which habitat stress causes disease and social pathology. Physiologists wonder how life is possible in habitat extremes. How can the eland and oryx of Africa, and the pocketmouse of Idaho, live without drinking? How can a mallard fly in the thin, cold air of 21,000 feet above sea level? How does the smallest of mammals, the bamboo bat, weighing an eighteenth of an ounce, maintain its body warmth? What colors do men see that birds and mammals do not? Students of the evolution of intelligence are captivated by the Galapagos woodpecker-finch that uses a thorn as a prizing tool, the Egyptian vulture that hurls a rock to break an ostrich egg, and the sea otter that uses a stone hammer to break the shell of a crab.

Perhaps the purest values in bird-and-beast watching are found in its symbolism. Humans have always lived closely with animals; our folklore and our speech are rich in animal characters. Is there perhaps some fundamental reason, bordering on instinct, that leads us to teach our children the spoken word through animal stories? The simple thought processes and reactions of Peter Rabbit, Reddy Fox, and the Three Little Pigs are completely understandable to children, while the behavior of adult people often is not. No matter that the picture-book beasts are imaginary and impossible, they act out parables in which the child can see himself among the players. More important, they suggest the continuum of life. Adults seldom entirely lose a mystical attachment to animals, though perhaps only to children can we admit this attachment and confess that the wild things of the world assuage our human loneliness.

I have heard grown men who entertain beliefs of this kind called "Bambi syndromers," men unable to see wild animals in a true light. They are sentimental. They lack that toughness of moral fiber which a man must have if he is to pull the trigger on Bambi and his numerous companions of the forest.

Ted Walker writes about whales:

> Where the seas are open moor
> and level blue, limitless,
> and swells are as soft grasses
> rolling over with the wind,
> often to the idleness
> of Azorean summer
>
> come the great whales. Long granites
> grow, slowly awash with sun,
> and waves lap along black skin
> like the shine of a laving
> rain upon a city pavement.
> Together they come, yet alone
> they seem to lie. Massively
> still, they bask, breathing like men.[15]

As art leads the artist to experiment, so the study of nature leads its devotees to search for new ways of appreciating and interacting with wildlife. Ornithologists Roger Tory Peterson and James Fisher compete in friendly fashion for the largest list of bird species seen in one year, and Fisher wins with 718.[16] Duck lovers collect the special stamps sold by the federal government to finance its waterfowl restoration program. Surely the oddest method of "birding" is to identify songs or calls heard on television. (Some calls are dubbed in by the producer, others are ad-libbed by uninvited birds in outdoor settings.)

Wolf lovers cooperate to capture the language and

music of wolves; the results are sound recordings of tremendous imaginative power. In Algonquin Park, Ontario, visitors are invited into the forest for "howling nights," when recordings are broadcast in order to bring responses from living wolves. A photographer specializes in "sets" of birds—that is, images of the nest and eggs, then the fledglings, and then the adults. A naturalist with a hobby that I find particularly attractive is a retired gentleman who goes out with an easy chair and quietly sits beside some animal trail—all day long if necessary—until a mink, fox, or rabbit comes by and then snaps a candid photo. A simple scheme, though ingenious.

Then there are the many thousands of men and women who find challenge in attracting birds and beasts to feeders and shelters, or in setting broken bones, or in washing oil from victims of the Age of Petroleum. The Quakers would say that these gentle people are giving testimony.

≯

IN February 1973 I spent a delightful week as scientific leader of a tour to waters and islands off the west coast of Baja California. Sponsored by Smithsonian Associates, the tour enabled thirty men and women from all walks of life to see marine birds and mammals in their native breeding haunts. The tour gave me a close look at a new kind of bird-and-beast watching—the photographic safari, or programmed wilderness adventure. Such safaris are a logical outgrowth, on the one hand, of diminishing wildlife populations near home and, on the other, of new and easy modes of travel, new outdoor recreation equipment, and, I believe, a recent switch in public interest from ordinary sightseeing to a more purposeful kind of outdoor travel. Many of the wildlife safari goers, on their return to civilization, do something positive for conservation.

On the trip to the Baja coast we came within touching distance of elephant seals—2-ton monsters with wrinkled faces, beasts from another age. We came within easy camera distance of harbor seals and their nursing pups, Guadalupe fur seals and California sea lions, and scores of gray whales, mating or nursing pairs. Less than 20 feet from their flashing bodies, I photographed three dolphins herding fish into the surf where I was standing. The gray whales were cruising in Scammon's Lagoon, the secret, shallow, inland place where Captain C. M. Scammon first found them in the winter of 1857–1858. Our party was one of several dozen groups that visited the lagoon in the winter of 1972–1973.

I hiked over volcanic trails lined with spring flowers and ran barefoot over white sand dunes a hundred feet high and saw gulls and pelicans wheeling against the dark blue sky. I was carried back to a time when the shores of my native land, too, were clean, and I thought, How wonderful to recapture a week of lost, young America!

More soberly, I know as a naturalist that the special

sort of bird-and-beast watching that our party was enjoying cannot be sustained without destroying the wildlife itself. The shy harbor seals and the brown pelicans and the other wild things have chosen, so to speak, to live in remote places for the very fact of their remoteness. People can only be intruders into the finely balanced, ritualized breeding activities of such animals.

One of our party in 1973 was an ornithologist who had visited San Martin Island twenty-five years earlier and had then counted 200 nesting pairs of pelicans. Now the nests were empty, long unused. He concluded that repeated disturbance by human visitors was the most likely reason for the disappearance of the birds. Not DDT, a notorious bird killer in waters farther north, since San Martin is little touched by agricultural poisons.

I am optimistic that Mexico will place controls on tourism in order to preserve the native wildlife and yet allow it to be seen. Guadalupe Island and Scammon's Lagoon have already been set aside as legal sanctuaries for the protection of breeding seals and whales. (Our party was allowed to enter them on a special science-education permit.) Along with whatever controls are placed on visitor disturbance to wildlife, there must be public education in wildlife biology. Visitors must know that wild creatures, especially in their breeding seasons, have strong needs for privacy and personal space. A wildlife safari should not be planned as a visit to a zoo.

PART TWO

WILDLIFE MANAGEMENT AND HOW IT WORKS

CHAPTER 10

The Administrative Structure

FORTY years ago, Charles Elton, a British zoologist, said: "The aim of most ecological studies of game birds, wild mammals, etc., is to find some means of eliminating fluctuations and maintaining as high a density as is practicable."[1] That is roughly the aim of wildlife management today—toward a sort of useful abundance of animals. Though management has also become deeply involved with public attitudes and preferences, it has remained essentially a numbers game.

The Wildlife Management Institute, in a statement endorsed by the National Wildlife Federation, the Wildlife Society, the American Humane Association, and the National Rifle Association, recently defined wildlife management as "the collection and application of biological information for the purposes of increasing and maintaining the numbers of animals within species and populations . . . at the optimum carrying capacity of their habitat. Management includes the entire scope of activities that constitute a modern scientific resource program, including, but not limited to, research, census, law enforcement, and habitat acquisition and improvement." [2]

I myself would define wildlife management as the process by which closely related needs of wild animals and of people are evaluated, reconciled, and met. It can be visualized as a flow chart in which facts and ideas enter the process and actions toward wildlife and people emerge (see chart).

By precedent based on old English law, wildlife in the United States is the property of the people, the sovereignty of which they have vested in the state.[3] No animal may be reduced to private ownership except by permission of the state. Wild animals do not belong to the owner of the land upon which the animals live, though the owner can post his land against entry and thus restrain the public from using its property. Outside the United States, ownership of wild animals is generally vested either in the nation or in the landowner, and responsibility for management is national.

Each of the fifty states makes its own classification of wildlife. The following scheme, used in the State of

THE FLOW OF OPERATIONS
IN WILDLIFE MANAGEMENT

Biologists estimate the populations of animals and study the life histories of individual species— which amounts to **LEARNING ABOUT WILDLIFE**	Sociologists and economists sample public attitudes and preferences with respect to wildlife uses— which amounts to **LEARNING ABOUT PEOPLE**

The resulting facts and ideas feed into

AN ADMINISTRATIVE STRUCTURE   of state and federal agencies having   legal responsibility for wildlife

The administrative structure acts by

DEALING WITH WILDLIFE indirectly, by manipulating habitats, or directly, by arranging for hunting seasons, controlling nuisance animals, raising animals on game farms, and exporting or importing animals	**DEALING WITH PEOPLE** by educating the public in wildlife conservation, by advising legislators and courts of law, by enforcing game laws, by training conservation workers, and by negotiating with landowners

139

Washington, is mainly a legal rather than a natural classification. For each category, two examples are given.

Birds
    Migratory Game Birds—ducks and mourning doves
    Upland Game Birds—ruffed grouse and wild turkey
    Non-protected Game Birds—house sparrow and starling
    Protected Birds [all others]—eagles and songbirds

Other Wildlife
    Protected Wildlife—grizzly bear and turtles
    Game Animals—native deer and bullfrog
    Furbearing Animals—muskrat and weasels
    Protected Marine Mammals—whales and seals
    Non-protected Animals—coyotes and mice

At the core of wildlife management is the administrative structure—the state and federal agencies which are legally responsible for wildlife. The federal government has gradually taken away from the states responsibility for animals on national parks and reservations; for animals, such as ducks and whales, that migrate across state or national boundaries; for rare and endangered species, such as the red wolf and eagle; and for animals imported to or exported from the United States. In 1920 the Supreme Court upheld the right of the federal government to regulate migratory waterfowl, and in subsequent years the states have conceded that the federal government is in a better position than they to deal with wildlife problems of national scope.

The Administrative Structure

The body of law pertaining to federal-state responsibility for wildlife is continually changing, mainly because the Constitution says nothing directly about federal power over wildlife. The federal government puts itself in the wildlife business partly through the commerce clause of the Constitution (Article I, Section 8), under which it is charged with maintaining watershed quality so that downstream waters will remain open to navigation. If, on federal land, a state game department allows a serious imbalance to develop between deer and vegetation, and the soil begins to wash away, the federal government has the right to intervene. As the last resort in any argument between federal and state governments over the welfare of public land, the supremacy clause of the Constitution (Article 6, Section 2) upholds the national interest.

In practice, state and federal wildlife agencies cooperate with little more grumbling than one would expect in a joint enterprise involving a daughter state and a mother nation. The federal government regards its role as one of guidance, rather than direction. In 1972, it collected $41 million in taxes on sporting arms and ammunition, then turned the receipts back to the individual states. It specified, however, that $37 million were to be spent for wildlife restoration and $4 million for hunter-safety programs.

Above the national scene are international commissions and councils—governmental or quasi-governmental—responsible for studying wildlife problems and recommending solutions. The seals of North America are of interest to at least six groups: the North Pacific Fur Seal Commission, the International Commission for the Northwest Atlantic Fisheries, the International Council for the Exploration of the Sea, the International Biological Program, the International Union for the Conservation of Nature and Natural Resources, and the United Nations Food and Agricultural Organization.

However, wildlife management is also partly a private, nongovernmental process. A directory issued by the National Wildlife Federations lists 254 private organizations concerned in one way or another with the four main operations on the flow chart at the beginning of this chapter. There are many others. The Federation itself has 3 million members and affiliates.[4] Few state game commissioners would dare to open a hunting season on wolves in opposition to the national conservation groups. Conversely, the support of these groups is helpful to such men as Jim Brooks, commissioner of the Alaska Department of Fish and Game, who, over bitter opposition from local hunters, banned the shooting of wolves from aircraft. Wildlife-oriented organizations focus the energies of persons having mutual interests in action for conservation, humane treatment of animals, public education in wildlife values, public health biology, land-use planning, zoos and beast parks, and wildlife legislation.

It is important to realize that wildlife management in the United States is by no means a smooth-running operation. On the contrary, tremendously powerful interests are working today against the welfare of wild animals, and they are interests on which conventional management has had little influence. Wildlife managers do not operate in a laboratory with colleagues of their own choosing; they are thrown in with politicians, corporate agriculturists, and industrialists of many stripes and colors, some of whom put gross national product ahead of gross national good. More acres of America are covered by pavement than by wilderness. The multibillion-dollar petroleum industry is moving into operations that threaten to foul the wildlife habitats of Alaska and the inshore waters of the Pacific coast. With some exceptions, American wildlife exists today not because of management but in spite of it. The variety and abundance of wildlife are dependent on man's decisions on land use.[5]

Former Secretary of the Interior Stewart L. Udall puts it this way: "The destroyers of our time are not greedy trappers or 'market hunters'; they are 'good farmers' attempting to enlarge the yields of their farmlands, and captains of industry who are ecological ignoramuses, intent only on achieving new goals of gross production." [6]

Wildlife management will improve as those who work inside its machinery become aware of the great undercurrents of sociological change in America. Wildlife managers (including myself) tend to exaggerate our biological and technological influence. We ought to study wildlife, not only as a land product, but as a barometer of balance between a people and its world.

The management of wildlife is a human process and its ultimate purpose is human welfare. Any biologist engaged in the process ought, therefore, to be guided by his conscience as well as his biological expertise. In manipulating wildlife populations he will often be asked to choose between two options, both of which are zoologically sensible, but one of which offers greater long-time benefit to people. To the extent that he is wise enough to choose the latter, to that extent will he advance his profession.

Two of my friends—marine zoologists—wrote not long ago an article in which they state their intention to bypass the reason for management and move straight to its technology.

"It is not our concern in this paper to define for society why it should need to kill fur seals or any other animal. The need may be real, as with food supplies, or it may be frivolous, as with millinery or women's fur coats, or it may concern economics or native rights. Our concern, however, is with a strategy of exploitation which leaves basic resources in good shape, and which protects the aesthetic values that serve to make our world more livable. We choose not to engage the question of motivation." [7]

Their textual disclaimer notwithstanding, the use of the words "aesthetic" and "livable" shows that good biologists cannot be blind to social goals.

CHAPTER 11

Learning about Wildlife

LEARNING about wildlife is the job of biologists and biostatisticians. Part of the job is routine: counting, measuring, surveying, monitoring, and bookkeeping. The rest is basic biology—discovering the life histories of the individual species.

Rarely can the biologist count directly a whole population as he can the fifty whooping cranes which still survive outside captivity. Rather, he must count a fraction and use the result as an index of the whole. A biologist traveled by ship and airplane around Svalbard, the Norwegian territories in the Arctic Ocean, counting all the polar bears within his visual path. He saw 195 bears, ranging in abundance from 1 per 105 square kilometers to 1 per 59 square kilometers, and representing a total population of 1,500 to 1,900 bears. The biologist may mark individuals by tag or paint, release them, and later tally the percentage of marked individuals returned by hunters. He may count beaver houses and goose nests as indicators of population size. He may walk through a transect (sample area) of a forest and tally by species the birdcalls that he hears. He may analyze by statistical methods the age composition of the deer in hunter-kills. All these techniques and others give insight into population levels, or, which is more pertinent to management, into population trends.

In perfecting census methods, the biologist moves stepwise, first learning a little about the life of the animal, then applying to management what he has learned, then through management practice finding new ways of estimating numbers. It would do him no good to count ground squirrels without knowing that the mantled species goes underground in late fall for winter sleep, whereas the Columbian species disappears in late spring for summer sleep. To simplify the staggering job of research on any animal, he begins by examining the most critical needs in its life: food, shelter, breeding opportunity, and "space," that little-known psychological territory which most animals seem to require. He moves on to detailed studies of anatomy, physiology, behavior, and pathology. Though thick monographs have been written about many important wildlife species, among them white-tailed deer, beaver, Canada goose, coyote, and bobwhite quail, research still continues.

Thirty years ago I was sent by the United States

Learning about Wildlife

Fish and Wildlife Service to diagnose a strange affliction of muskrats in Tule Lake Refuge, California. The Service had an arrangement with local trappers for a share of the muskrat pelts taken from the refuge. One year, when the dried pelts arrived at the Seattle Fur Exchange about half were downgraded because they were torn or bitten. I tramped around Tule Lake in February, looking for signs of marauding birds or mammals, but found none. I followed a trapline with one of the local men, pushing through the brown rushes, following the trails of frozen mud made by the muskrats coming and going from their holes in the ice. We found several muskrats which had been partly eaten during the night while they were in the traps. Then I climbed upon a muskrat lodge and counted 150 such lodges within my circle of vision over a barren part of the lake where most of the rushes had been destroyed. I knew then that I was looking at an "eat-out." The population had irrupted, and the starving animals were eating their own kind, attacking first the helpless ones caught in traps.

I never went back to Tule Lake. Nowadays, biologists faced with a similar problem would press for an ecological study of the region. They would ask, Are mink and weasel—natural predators of the muskrat—also being removed by trapping? Are the hawks and owls, coyotes, bobcats, and foxes which normally live around such lakes being shot, trapped, or poisoned? Have activities of man modified the water-level and drainage relationships of the lake? And, finally, is wide fluctuation in numbers a characteristic of muskrat populations and therefore a thing to be accepted—indeed welcomed—as a natural phenomenon in a public wildlife refuge?

Biology, of course, can never come to the end of its scientific track; all biological reports end with the words, implicit or explicit: "These findings are preliminary . . . the problem needs further study." The more intense become pressures upon the biologist to supply answers, the more numerous become the questions.

On the basis of biology, wildlife management has been trying since 1950 to bring the Alaska fur seal herd up (or perhaps down?) to the level of maximum yield, but the herd is not responding. Three reasons have been postulated. Soviet and Japanese commercial fishing, which has greatly increased in recent years around the seal islands, is depleting the fish stocks upon which the mother seals depend during the summer breeding season. Pesticides and poisonous metals, found in the North Pacific Ocean and in the tissues of all seals examined so far, are indirectly lowering the food supply or the fertility rate of the seals. Certain management operations, especially the driving of pups in order to mark them, are resulting in increased mortality of young or decreased fertility of adults. There may be other reasons why the seals do not conform to the model predicted for them; the foregoing are the most likely.

I HAVE watched with great interest the growth of natural area preserves. These represent a rather new kind of land use, of increasing value to biologists. As of 1968, there were more than 300 preserves on United States federal lands alone.[1] The main reasons for setting them aside are, in the words of a Forest Service team: "To provide baseline areas against which the effects of human activities in similar environments can be measured, to provide sites for study of natural processes in undisturbed ecosystems, and to provide gene pool preserves for plant and animal species, particularly of rare and endangered types." [2]

From an inside position during the past fifteen years I have seen the development of a preserve system in the State of Washington. The push began among two task forces: professional biologists in colleges and laymen in the Nature Conservancy. Our efforts bore fruit in 1972 when the state established by law a system of preserves. The new law is a broad one, certain to please the public, which is in fact why the legislators could be persuaded to take land off the tax rolls. The law proclaims that: "natural lands, together with the plants and animals living thereon in natural ecological systems, are valuable for the purposes of scientific research, teaching, as habitats of rare and vanishing species, as places of natural historic and natural interest and scenic beauty, and as living museums of the original heritage of the state." [3]

By and large, nature preserves will never be popular with politicians; they call for withdrawing land from the tax base and for spending public funds to maintain special places which most of the public will never use. Conservationists insist, however, that abstract as well as monetary values must be considered in land planning. Because the meaning of ecology is now beginning to be appreciated by lawmakers, I believe that conservationists, for a few years to come, will have increasing success in persuading governments to establish preserves. Then perhaps a reaction will set in as suitable wild lands become scarcer. In the meantime, the strongest selling point for preserves is that they are lands for learning. Education is more sacred to lawmakers than are research, recreation, and aesthetic appreciation.

Some of us are privately pleased that parcels of wild land are being set aside, because we know that they hold hidden artistic and spiritual values. On a few islands off the coast of New Zealand there lives a reptile with an ancestry older than the dinosaur's. It is the tuatara—a baby dragon with a third eye overgrown with skin on the top of its head. It is one of the few reptiles with a true voice and has been heard to croak dolefully on misty nights. It can be lured from its burrow by music. When the New Zealand government set up a special preserve for the tuatara, American zoologist Archie Carr remarked, "I wish they had said it was not to placate zoologists, but so that plain men could go on singing the tuatara out of its hole." [4]

CHAPTER 12

Learning about People

WILDLIFE management tries to hold animal populations at the levels of greatest good for people. This means that someone has to decide which species will be favored over others, in what numbers and proportions, and in what localities. Decisions become daily more difficult as outdoor America becomes daily more artificial. Only that tiny fraction of the native fauna which survives in set-aside wilderness is unchanged from colonial times, and even that fraction is rained upon by industrial, domestic, and military poisons from moving currents of the air. The native bison have decreased in numbers from 60 million to 30,000, while the deer have increased from half a million to 15 million. Primitive America is a memory. Decisions for reconciling the life styles of people and the life styles of wild animals in a new and altered landscape must continually be made.

As a consequence, management requires input from people—it needs to know their attitudes and preferences. I suggested earlier that no wildlife issue will ever be settled fairly on the basis of biological findings alone; public sentiment has also to be considered.

At the level of the state game department, wildlife managers hear more opinions than they care for: opinions from hunters, trappers, and birdwatchers; opinions from irate farmers claiming damage by deer or beaver; opinions from owners of shooting grounds and bird-dog kennels. The steadiest flow of advice comes from local hunters who besiege the district warden or gather in the Grange hall with others of their kind to draft resolutions to the game director. This of course is grassroots America.

From time to time, a game department will initiate an inquiry, through questionnaire or interview, into hunter preferences. The returns are useful in indicating how the hunters want their game funds allocated: to the purchase of public hunting lands, to winter feeding of elk, to building trails into new hunting ranges, to securing easements for entry into private farmlands, to constructing hunting camp facilities, to controlling predators thought to be harmful to game, or to other activities.

A growing number of economists are interested in measuring the demand for and the value of sport-hunting, mainly to put hunting into the public arena where bidding for land use takes place. Another reason is to reveal which of the local recreation spots are the favorites, thereby providing management with incentive to improve the others. In Nevada, game managers increased the deer food on less-favored hunting areas by seeding them with crested wheatgrass and by removing "scrub" trees—pinyon and juniper. I report this "improvement" without liking it, for the pinyon-juniper lands, covering millions of acres in the Southwest, are ecologically fascinating.

Two methods of measuring recreational value are commonly used, one based on expenditures and the other on demand. Demand is the harder to estimate; it is calculated from a statistical curve which indicates the user's increasing reluctance to spend money for sport as its cost increases.

Precisely how nation-wide opinion can best be sampled as a guide to planning for wildlife conservation is a question that I am not prepared to answer. Millions of dollars are already being spent by such private polling firms as the Gallup Organization and the Opinion Research Corporation; the federal government is also taking polls through its Office of Management and Budget and its National Science Foundation.

Polls do not indicate where we should go, but only where we are going. They reflect mass mediocrity along with thoughtful appraisal; some are shortsighted, others prophetic. I do not suggest that majority opinion can be a complete guide to planning for wildlife conservation, but that its trend can be useful. Quite possibly a poll taken tomorrow would show majority support for the established historical concept, "wildlife equals game," though I feel sure that the majority would be smaller than it was in the 1960s. The direction of moving thought is what counts, not its momentary position.

An effort to improve the value of polls through a feedback system is currently being made by the Foreign Policy Association. Its Great Decisions program, sponsored by civic and religious organizations, schools and colleges, extension services, labor and farm groups, business corporations, newspapers and broadcasting stations, and libraries, offers educational material, then polls the opinions of those whom it has presumably educated. The Association (which was founded in 1918) conducts seminars and conferences, works with the mass media, and issues pamphlets and books. Though the process could become circular and counterproductive, it does in fact seem to develop an informed, thoughtful public opinion at the community level. It allows common information to be seen in the light of individual experience or individual cultural background. Something like it could serve as a model for assessment of national priorities with respect to wildlife uses and wildlife management.

Wildlife managers, and the hunters whom they principally serve, began only in the current decade to hear the voices of outsiders asking to share in decisions about wildlife use. During its forty years of existence, professional management has been weakened by in-breeding; in this respect it resembles the professions of education and medicine. The consequences are narrow vision, resistance to change, emphasis on structure at the expense of broad helpfulness, and a dwindling sense of humanity. The average wildlife manager understands many of the whats and hows but few of the whys of the process. However, because I see within the profession a core of individuals who understand what the new conservationists are talking about, I am encouraged to believe that the profession can be the agent for change to a more democratic system.

CHAPTER 13

Dealing with Wildlife through Habitats

MAN intervenes in the affairs of wild animals either by manipulating their habitats or by directly changing their numbers. Persons who give little thought to wildlife conservation may suppose that governments "preserve" animals by forbidding hunters to shoot them and by arresting poachers. In fact, the fate of wildlife depends heavily on land-use planning to provide habitats where animals can live and breed. Given space, an animal community will usually solve its own biological problems.

At the level of American suburbia, millions of homeowners are trying to preserve habitats for the wild birds and mammals which they have known from childhood as bright accessories to life. The National Audubon Society sells a do-it-yourself book on habitat improvement, the text of which vibrates with the modern spirit of organic gardening. It crawls and oozes with fertility. (Living in harmony with nature was recognized as right for wild creatures long before it was recognized as right for people.) The book gives sixty recipes for upgrading lands and waters for wildlife, recipes which I summarize and regroup here according to the vital needs which they satisfy.[1]

Do not manicure the land, say the Audubon writers, but provide "edge," a magic word that means variety: long ragged lines of contact between evergreens and deciduous plants; strip gardens; woodlot openings maintained by selective cutting; and, in short, everything that monoculture eliminates. The resulting patchwork will have buffering capacity against sudden changes or natural disasters. The concept of edge is familiar to bird-watchers—and to hunters as well. Both know that, along edge, the chances are best of finding richness in numbers and variety.

Plant native foods—grasses, shrubs, and trees useful to wildlife—and cut back plant species that occupy valuable space but do not contribute seeds, berries, or nuts. Around my own country place I have thinned out the willow, alder, and bigleaf maple in favor of salal, Oregon grape, vine maple, Indian plum, kinnikinnick, native apple, cascara, osier, wild rose, snowberry, and hazelnut. My driveway would doubtless be smoother if it were blacktop, but its fine-crushed rock provides grit for quail.

Ways to provide water will vary with the nature

of the country, whether arid or moist. A siphon, like the kind in a chicken watering trough, will run from a reservoir for months without attention. In the dry desert foothills of the Southwest I have seen "guzzlers" built by game managers—concrete aprons to catch the infrequent rains and store their waters in a tank drained by siphon. Waterfowl, muskrats, mink, and other aquatic species prefer ponds which do not fluctuate. The water level can be stabilized by earth dams, dikes, and canals. A sustained water level provides nesting and denning places and subirrigates permanent vegetation around the shore. The fluctuating level, or drawdown, which is characteristic of large reservoirs is not only ugly but repels wildlife. The latter disadvantage is often ignored by water engineers, who speak in glowing words of the "recreational wildlife" to be gained from a new reservoir.

Cover, in the form of living plants, brush and rock piles, and fallen trees, meets an instinctive need for shelter from enemies. I make "chipmunkeries" by piling armfuls of fir bark, later to be tunneled by small mammals.

Nesting requirements for wildlife can be met by leaving hollow stumps, thickets, rotten wood, and, in general, the stuff that land developers attack as unsightly. The Audubon advisers are fond of putting up artificial houses for birds, squirrels, and raccoons, which is next best when the natural hidey-holes have been lost. Few of us are privileged to leave rotten logs in our front yards, and those who do are doubtless breaking some civilized law.

Dealing with Wildlife through Habitats

Finally, wild animals need loafing room, personal space for preening, sunning themselves, and dusting their feathers or fur. A robin gets a squirmy sort of pleasure from soaking in the hot sun on a pile of bark, wings outspread, sprawled on its belly as though it recalled the posture of a reptilian ancestor.

⩔

EVERY farmer knows that the Audubon program is right in pointing to the basic values of soil and water conservation and plant complexity for the production of wildlife. It does not follow that the farmer will provide for wildlife at the expense of losing arable land or having robins eat his cherries. This is unfortunate, since the farmers of America could be the most important wildlife managers in the country. We pay them to produce food, not pleasant countryside; they give us food and also landscapes that are prairielike, biologically uninteresting, and aesthetically sterile. I do not suggest providing farmers with a subsidy for producing wildlife, a device that could lead to the dole, but I think they might be offered tax relief in return for easements to their land. In such cases the farmers would agree to allow public access in certain areas, to maintain footpaths, and to encourage the growth of trees, shrubs, and aquatic plants attractive to wildlife.

The United States Department of Agriculture is, in fact, toying with a "Set-Aside Program" which calls for public access to private farmlands. During 1972, $1,500,000 were allocated to pay 5,000 farmers in ten states. The selected farmers agreed to permit free public access to their lands for hunting, fishing, trapping, or hiking.[2]

The legal and moral implications of the federal program are not altogether clear; it is likely to be challenged in a class-action suit. A conscientious objector to the killing of wild animals for sport may protest, "I don't want my tax money used to subsidize that activity, and when I take my children to a Set-Aside pond to look at waterfowl, I don't want to dodge gunfire." A duck hunter, on the other hand, may demand, "What the hell are those kids doing, scaring the ducks!"

The potential wildlife value of farmland now lying idle is enormous. Federal crop-surplus plans and diversion programs go back to the 1930s. In recent years the Department of Agriculture has been paying farmers about $3 billion a year for not growing crops. If federal subsidies are to continue (I am not saying they should), how much better it would be to allocate some of them toward restoring wildlife cover on idle, eroding lands.

❧

THE best wildlife habitats of America are those on the great federal holdings, followed in quality by those on state preserves, and then by private farmlands which contain woodlots, hedgerows, thickets, poplar bottoms, ponds, and other places attractive to animals. The federal lands of the United States total 755 million acres. They are controlled as follows: Bureau of Land Management, 62 percent; Forest Service, 25 percent; Department of Defense, 4 percent; Fish and Wildlife Service, 4 percent; National Park Service, 3 percent; other agencies, 2 percent. The lands are unevenly distributed—about 50 percent in Alaska, 45 percent in the eleven western states, and only 5 percent in all the central, southern, and eastern states combined.[3]

The purest habitats are those portions of the national parks preserved in the Wilderness System established in 1964. Forbidden here are hunting; trapping; logging; mining; the use of poisons, pesticides, and herbicides; and motor vehicles. Even airplanes are forbidden above the Quetico-Superior Lake system.

Sport-hunting is permitted in only one of the national park wilderness areas, Grand Teton. When that park was created in 1950, the state of Wyoming reserved the right to manage game species within its boundaries. Here the fiction is maintained that hunting for elk is a reduction program and a management tool, rather than recreation.

Outside of their wilderness pockets, the national parks are deteriorating. The Conservation Foundation (founded in 1947) has recently released a report sharply critical of the Park Service for allowing its lands to become citified; cluttered with roads, parking lots, dogs and cats, concessions, trailer camps, shopping centers, automobiles, motorcycles, motorboats, sightseeing planes, and helicopters.[4] The Service replies that the parks are

for the people, though its voice is barely audible above the public din. If certain recommendations of the Foundation are followed, the parks will slowly regain the precious qualities for which they were set aside in the first place. People will visit a park on its terms rather than theirs.

Even if the Park Service were to be given a free hand to restore natural conditions, it would still face the task of re-educating a generation of park visitors. Tourists from the city have been conditioned to think of a national park as a magnified safari land, like those man-made creations erupting across the country from California to New Jersey. A national park, according to the average American visitor, is a place where one feeds chocolate-coated peanuts to squirrels. For him, the image of a park as a place where one should not be sure of encountering a deer, bear, or marten, and thus be correspondingly thrilled if one does, is now too sophisticated. None the less, I believe that public thought should gently be nudged toward that image. Though the fact is little known, the national parks of the American continent, created from virgin wilderness, are unique in world history. Their management and evolution are being watched by naturalists all over the world. Planning for their future should conserve the clarity of purpose it had in the beginning.

≽

THE National Wildlife Refuge System, like the National Park Service, is run by the Department of the Interior.

In 1903, President Theodore Roosevelt set aside Pelican Island in Florida to protect nesting pelicans, herons, and egrets from molestation by hunters and fishermen. From that beginning there has grown a system of refuges containing 30 million acres of land and water. These are not sanctuaries; all are integrated with other uses. They serve as resting, feeding, and breeding places for hundreds of kinds of wild animals, though mainly for ducks and geese. Increasingly they serve as national barometers—controlled areas where biologists can look for changes in pollution levels, in the populations of migratory waterfowl, and in visitor attitudes toward wildlife. The refuges harbor twenty-seven of the wildlife forms listed in the *Federal Register* as endangered species.

Although the Refuge System is now seventy years old, it had no very clear policy until 1970, when the Leopold Committee of 1968 pushed it into stating its mission as one "to provide, manage, and safeguard a national network of lands and waters sufficient in size, diversity, and location to insure the protection of wildlife of all types, and to provide environments in which human relationships with land and wildlife are encouraged." [5]

The refuge managers seem to have chronic difficulty in assigning relative importance to the various roles of their lands as sanctuaries, as duck factories, as outdoor schools and laboratories, and as public wildlife displays. The confused scenario is reflected in the variety of engineered landscaping which one sees on the refuges.

Dealing with Wildlife through Habitats

Some lands are kept natural; others are dammed, diked, channeled, seeded to exotic plants, and forested or deforested.

The refuges were conceived as sanctuaries, but the first one was opened to hunting in 1924 and the others by 1958. The liberalization came through congressional action, and I suspect that the managing agency itself may have been embarrassed by it. In the twenty pages of the publication, *National Wildlife Refuges, 1970,* hunting is mentioned only once, in a table showing that 3.2 percent of the visitor use in 1970 was by hunters.[6] I also suspect that some donors do not fully understand that the so-called refuges are required by law to serve also as sport-shooting grounds. Otherwise, how could the Rachel Carson Refuge on the coast of Maine have been dedicated, after her death, to that gentle person who once wrote, "We cannot have peace among men whose hearts find delight in killing any living creature"?[7]

In the fall of 1972 I visited the Finley Refuge, a 5,000-acre jewel in the Willamette Valley of Oregon. It is the most important single winter haven for the dusky Canada geese, which nest in summer in Alaska. Signs on the refuge ask the visitor please to stay in his car, because the geese may mistake any person on foot for a hunter and rise in panic. I could understand the danger, for shooting is allowed not only on the refuge but on the adjacent farmland, posted as private shooting ground.

At times when the hunting season is closed within a national wildlife refuge and open outside the fence, concentrations of wildlife are especially vulnerable. During one season at Sand Lake Refuge, South Dakota, 1500 hunters surrounded the sanctuary in one day. They reported an all-season kill of 36,000 geese and estimated that 20,000 others were crippled or killed but not retrieved.

Would it not be feasible to establish buffer zones around the federal refuges—greenbelts or farmlands where only compromise disturbance would be tolerated? Would it not indeed be feasible to bind all future land donations to the refuge system by a reverter clause which would bar the use of donated lands for hunting?

Many conservationists are pushing for expansion of the refuge system while reserving the right to criticize its management. They feel that dollar considerations should have less influence. In 1970 the government took in $4,300,000 from refuge sales or leases—gas and oil royalties, forest products, grass and hay, surplus animals, public-use concessions, furs, and sand and gravel. Many believe that refuges ought to be such in fact, as well as in name, free from hunting and trapping, oil drilling and mining, and forestry and agriculture (except perhaps the raising of special crops to provide food for wintering birds).

Wildlife management on national lands should relate to broad national attitudes and preferences. In the public mind, a refuge is equivalent to a preserve or sanctuary. It is a place where men, women, and children come quietly on foot, any day in the year, to see wild animals at home. The people have a spiritual as well as a material investment in their refuges. Any kind of management which fails to recognize the national mood deserves to fail.

The fact that the refuges were partly paid for by taxes collected from hunters is irrelevant. Again, the concern of the new conservationists is less with history than with seeing that the original purpose of the refuges is reinstated, that they serve the public interest, that they serve the needs of all elements of society. Purchase of the refuges as a spin-off result of the sale of guns and ammunition will be seen as a mistake if it leads to increased use of the refuges for hunting. Bird-and-beast watchers, searching in America for unafraid, unhunted forms of wildlife, will find them rare, for the best land and water habitats will have been taken up for shooting grounds.

THUS far the discussion of animal habitats has dealt with making them attractive to wildlife. There is however, another reason for manipulating habitats and that is to make them unattractive to animals which are endangering man's interests.

Hitting at animals through their environment is one form of biocontrol, the control of life with life. Just as public health authorities would rather prevent an epidemic than to cope with it afterward, so wildlife managers would rather prevent the rise of animal numbers to nuisance levels than handle the problems which that rise would cause.

Controlling animals through habitat is dynamically efficient; it forces the animals to pay out of their own energy stores for the reduction of their own numbers. It is self-sustaining; it does not call for recurrent expense. It does not provoke within the nuisance animal the kind of genetic counterattack which is seen in wild rat populations exposed for generations to poisons. Though rats become "fast" (resistant) to poisons, they do not become fast to living competitors evolving with them in a sort of armament race. Because a biocontrolled system is always complex—rich in predator-prey, competitor, and symbiont relationships—single populations within it have little chance of attaining nuisance numbers. When a population of field mice begins to rise, various internal or genetic governors, as well as external ones, begin to depress the birthrate, while hawks, owls, and foxes move in to raise the death rate. Moreover, biocontrol does not contaminate, whereas conventional wildlife poisons carry destruction far outside the target area.

Conservationists find biocontrol through habitat especially attractive. They have learned to trust and respect natural systems, those that have evolved through cosmic trial and error, those that are here today because they work. Conservationists doubt the wisdom and even the sincerity of chemical industry lobbyists who promise a world controlled through poisons. The power of advertising money is too strong; the testimony of *Silent Spring* is still too plain.[8]

Sadly for our present generation, biocontrol through habitat as a wildlife management tool is poorly understood and therefore little used. Management is largely the job of governments, and governments operate from one crisis to the next, forever under pressure for quick and cheap solutions. Biocontrol calls for long preliminary study of the ecosystem and is expensive until it becomes operant. By cultural habit, Americans are more apt to think vaguely of outdoor ecosystems as some sort of "parks" than as real mediums for the biocontrol of bird and mammal pests.

The value of biocontrol through habitat can best be illustrated by some examples. The ungulates, or hoofed animals, in those national parks large enough to be ecologically complete are, without control by man, doing nicely and are not abusing their habitats. In this category are the moose of Grand Teton, the elk of Yellowstone, one of the bison herds of Yellowstone, and the elk and mule deer of Glacier. On the Hanford Reservation, comprising 600 square miles of sagebrush country in eastern Washington, no hunting of any kind has been permitted since 1943, and in the ensuing thirty years, neither the populations of native deer nor those of their predators have irrupted.

A man who raises fancy ducks in Missouri was losing about ten birds a year to great horned owls, though he shot owls at every opportunity. Then he decided to capitalize on a bit of behavioral information: horned owls are strongly territorial and will drive away others of their kind. He began to shoot to scare rather than to kill. One pair of owls continued to nest nearby, though avoiding his pond, and this pair kept other owls from invading. He lost only one duck in the next two years.

Deliberate introduction of a pathogen into the environment to control a wildlife population has, I believe, been tried only with the myxoma virus. This virus is native to the Americas, and American rabbits are genetically resistant to it. It was introduced into France in 1952 through the inoculation of two rabbits. It spread rapidly in western Europe and to Great Britain, killing about 90 percent of the native rabbits. The Old World rabbits will eventually develop a degree of immunity, though the virus will continue to dampen irruptions in their populations.

Although the thought of encouraging, let alone introducing, predatory animals as agents of biocontrol will cause the average old-time game manager to bristle, it is an idea whose time has come. An ideal test site would be a commercial second-growth forest which is losing tree seeds and seedlings to rabbits and rodents, and from which coyotes and bobcats are being eliminated by man. If the carnivores were allowed to increase to the limits imposed by the environment, there would be fewer grouse and perhaps fewer deer for the sportsmen, but there would also be fewer small-mammal pests.

Some years ago farmers of Santa Clara Valley, California, were losing annually about $40,000 worth of gladioli plantings to "cottontails." A biologist pointed out that the offending animals were in fact brush rabbits and that these instinctively remain near shelter. When the farmers cut back the brush within 45 feet of their plantings, they had no more trouble from rabbits.

Biologists at Horicon Marsh, Wisconsin, found that the average Canada goose will not reach higher than 38 inches to feed on growing corn. Today, where farmers grow corn in the path of migrating geese, they are advised to grow strains that ear-out at a greater height. Conversely, if a refuge manager is growing corn intended for waterfowl feed, he is advised to raise low-growing strains.

Experiments have been carried on for many years in the United States and Canada in maintaining attractant plots of grains or pasture grasses to lure birds away from valuable crops. Though the method is effective on the blueprint, it is not always economical in application.

Gulls, though enjoyed for their beauty, and the poetry of their flight, and their contribution to best-selling books, can be harmful. They are a strike hazard to aircraft; they carry filth from garbage dumps and sewer outfalls to reservoirs; on nature preserves they eat the eggs and young of auks, murres, puffins, petrels, shearwaters, avocets, and terns. Though many ways are known of reducing gull populations directly by killing the birds or their embryos, biocontrol through habitat is still experimental. Gull numbers have been reduced by cleaning up fish landing docks and animal farms, by incinerating rubbish, and by treating sewage. Foxes and raccoons (of one sex only) have been placed on small gull-nesting islands, though not on islands where other, more valuable seabirds are also nesting. Alongside the runway of a certain airfield, the grass was allowed to grow tall in order to discourage gulls, which it did. But starlings increased; one set of nuisance birds was replaced by another. Moreover, the tall grass encouraged field mice, which in turn attracted raptorial birds. The grass also encouraged earthworms, which then crawled out on the airstrip on rainy nights and attracted gulls! Such interrelationships illustrate the vexing difficulties of biocontrol through habitat.

An offbeat kind of biocontrol is based on the scarecrow principle—the introduction of an imitation enemy. In the Kvichak River of Alaska, millions of young red salmon come down every spring on their way to the sea. They are met by hungry belugas, or white whales, in numbers from 50 to 500. Because the red salmon is a valuable commodity, the Alaska Department of Fish and Game has been trying for years to repel the belugas before they have a chance to enter the mouth of the river to feed on little fish. Department employees chased the belugas in motorboats, dropped dynamite charges among them, and finally played high-intensity underwater sounds—the recorded voices of killer whales. On the first trial, the belugas turned immediately at the sound and swam out of the river against an incoming tide. Later, they learned to cross the 2-mile-wide river and sneak upstream in waters where the playback signals were weaker. The most recent plan of the researchers is to place a sound projector on each side of the river during the three weeks each year when the salmon are migrating.

Recorded distress calls have been used to frighten starlings, blackbirds, and crows. When crows can be driven from their nests on a few cold nights, the eggs chill, and a generation of crows is lost. The effectiveness of sonic devices increases the more faithfully they mimic the dialect of the target flock. It is no use trying to scare a Nebraska starling with a voice recorded in Bronx Park.

Even more sophisticated than noise devices are chemical agents that create "living scarecrows." Certain harmless drugs, concealed in bait, will put birds to sleep or produce fluttering and flapping symptoms that cause other birds in the flock to leave the baited areas in dismay.

This discussion has drifted from self-sustaining or feedback control to control by repeated input from man. There is no hard line between the two, but the first approach is the more desirable and should receive in the future a greater share of experiment and funding than it has in the past.

CHAPTER 14

Dealing with Wildlife Directly

WILDLIFE management aims to shape animal populations to fit them to human demands. That aim is implicit in the policy of the Washington State Game Department—"to provide the maximum amount of wildlife-oriented recreation for the people." [1] The Game Department, in the process of changing animal numbers, spends $2 million or $3 million a year on direct methods—killing, capturing, and translocating—for every million it spends on indirect methods—manipulating habitats.

Foremost among direct methods are arrangements with hunters and trappers which result in the killing of specified numbers of animals each year. Ideally, the numbers represent the net natural reproduction, or net increase. Up to 40 percent of a deer population can ordinarily be killed each winter—a lower percentage if only trophy sized bucks are taken, a higher percentage if both sexes and young animals are taken. Game departments establish hunting and trapping seasons by time and locality, by species, by qualification of the licensee, and by specification of his hunting equipment. They tell him when he must use a guide and they examine the credentials of the guide.

Some departments arrange to move hunters into remote country. They may arrange with a tree-farm owner in the mountains for free transportation of hunters and their kill. Most states contract with farmers for easements onto farmlands during the hunting season. The hunters benefit thereby, while the lands are less likely to be abused by hunters than if they were bluntly posted KEEP OUT!

A second way in which game departments put direct pressure on wildlife is by controlling nuisance animals through shooting, trapping, poisoning, gassing, digging out dens, destroying nests, or inhibiting reproduction by means of drugs. They may capture individuals alive and move them, as they did the beaver that wandered onto the Seattle Arboretum a few years ago. In the Washington Game Department, the allotment for animal control is about 5 percent of the total budget. Control operations mollify the hunter, for whom wild carnivores represent competition, and pacify the farmer, the livestock owner, and the suburbanite whose interests are damaged in one way or another by wildlife.

Ira Gabrielson tells a story that seems to show that killing predators may be desirable when they threaten a rare game species. In northwestern Nevada, a little band of antelope, though protected from hunting, was not increasing in numbers. The United States Biological Survey undertook to control the local predators, and during the next thirteen years its men killed 7,595 coyotes and bobcats. Concurrently, the antelope increased from 500 to at least 7,000.[2] Assuming that other factors limiting population growth, such as disease, stormy weather, poor food supply, poisonous plants, accidents, and illegal hunting, were constant during the thirteen years, predator control would seem to have been justified as first aid to an endangered stock.

At the upper end of a reservoir in Oklahoma, about 10 million crows spend the winter on a patch of land called the Fort Cobb Game Management Area. Many of the crows fly north in spring to nest in the central provinces of Canada. From September to March, thousands of sportsmen hunt crows at Fort Cobb and on the nearby farmlands, where peanuts and cotton are grown. Some hunter groups come from outside the state to spend a week shooting crows and more crows. Though I have not visited Fort Cobb or polled the opinions of natives there, the present arrangement seems to be an acceptable way of controlling a species where it is damaging agriculture. Shooting crows for fun is unlikely to get out of hand, for the birds are migratory species regulated by federal as well as state law.

Dealing with Wildlife Directly

Dealing with peak populations of animals which destroy trees and shrubs is a perennial problem on public lands; such species include goats, deer, elk, porcupine and beaver. In Hawaii Volcanoes National Park, wild goats, descendants of those introduced in the eighteenth century, are exterminating native plants and causing the soft volcanic soil to erode. More than 70,000 goats have been killed or removed alive from the park. Park managers believe that every one of the goats will have to be removed, which will entail the construction of more than 100 miles of fencing on terrain bathed in lingering dampness and corrosive volcanic fumes, a stepped-up program of killing and driving, and the introduction of trained goat dogs handled by park rangers.

At present, the park managers encourage what they call "local citizen participation in the reduction and disposal of excess goats." Local hunters are "deputized" as park employees. After signing a permit which releases the government from responsibility for their actions, they are allowed to hunt without supervision. In 1972 they killed 1,917 goats, as against 1,616 killed or caught alive by park rangers. The park managers admit that present methods of control are unsatisfactory. They say that the take of goats is not as important as the untaken remainder.[3]

Anthony Wayne Smith, president of the National Parks and Conservation Association, disapproves of the Park Service program. "The use of sports hunters . . . is, in our judgment, a sports hunting program, not a

177

legitimate management program. It is also directed toward the wrong objective, maintenance of the goat populations, not their elimination." [4]

My own feeling is that the Park Service, chronically underfinanced and chronically pressured by local—as against national—interests, has taken the easy way out in Hawaii. I am sure that many of its staff members would have preferred to follow the recommendations of its own Leopold Committee of 1963:

"Every phase of management itself [should] be under the full jurisdiction of biologically trained personnel of the Park Service. This applies not only to habitat manipulation but to all facets of regulating animal populations. Reducing the numbers of elk in Yellowstone or of goats on Haleakala Crater is part of an over-all scheme to preserve or restore a natural biotic scene. The purpose is single-minded." [5]

Conservationists were horrified to learn in 1971 that the owners of at least nine ranches in Colorado and Wyoming had taken wildlife control into their own hands; they had hired gunmen to shoot golden eagles and bald eagles from a helicopter. About 800 of those protected birds were slain in a private war declared by sheepmen who claimed that the birds were preying upon lambs. Later the criminals were given a slap on the wrist in federal court; two were fined $500 each and one $1,700.

In the fall of 1972, an official of the Province of Quebec announced that the first fifty persons to deliver a dead wolf or coyote to the Fish and Game Branch would receive a "handsome trophy." The trophy? "The jaw of the wolf . . . set in an acrylic block with the hunter's name inscribed upon it." [6] Not the name of the wolf—the name of its killer. In this fashion did the government launch a program which called, first, for obtaining wolf specimens for scientific study, then for setting out 600 wolf traps to mop up the survivors. Letters of outrage descended upon the official and upon the Queen of England (who was presumed to have influence upon him). Those who wrote were upset by the prospect that animals symbolic of the vanishing Canadian wilderness were about to be destroyed. I suppose there were also some who disliked the idea that killers could be hired for a piece of bone embedded in plastic. No harm seems to have been done in the wolf caper except to official dignity. By early 1973, only six wolves had been killed and only one hunter had qualified for a trophy; the government withdrew its offer.

There is a trend in wildlife control away from the payment of "bounties," a scalping reward, and toward the use of biocontrol methods. For twenty-eight years the State of South Dakota paid average annual bounties on more than 15,000 foxes; in 1972 it paid bounties on 22,000. The system is evidently keeping the animals near their level of maximum productivity, which was not in the original plan. The bounty philosophy is punitive and nonselective; it implies that all foxes in South Dakota are harmful. And it ignores the feelings of citizens who like to see a fox now and then, though it may please the hunters who do not like to see a fox carrying the body of a pheasant.

The advantages of using antifertility drugs (chemisterilants) to hold animal numbers at low levels have been explained by a federal scientist. First, he writes, "it may be more practical to prevent animals from being born than to reduce their numbers after they are partially or fully grown and established in a secure environment." Second, when outright poisons are used, the animals that escape suddenly find themselves in an uncrowded environment, and their reproductive rate jumps. Given the choice, then, of increasing an animal's death rate or decreasing its birth rate, the latter is the wise one. Third, many poisons are unpalatable, or the animal develops a distaste for them. By their very nature, antifertility drugs are insidious, "friendly to the body," and acceptable. Fourth, chemisterilants are more humane than poisons.[7]

In my opinion, the public would rather visualize a coyote living out a long, though indeed loveless life than one writhing in the agony of cardiac-respiratory failure as a result of poison.

The control of bird and mammal pests should be ecologically sound, economic, and socially acceptable. When, in the future, the ecology of natural regulation is better understood, control methodology in compatibility with both environment and animal will suggest itself. We Americans ought to accept a certan amount of damage from animals as we do damage from hail, dust, and lightning—with tolerance. According to two spokesmen for the Wildlife Society, "Modern civilized man assumes that his hypersensitivity to pest situations will always be resolved in his favor through technology, laws, or force. It is a false assumption. More and more, as the usable space for livelihood decreases through population growth, we will be required to live with our self-imposed pest situations. To do otherwise may be impossible, for there will be few acceptable alternatives." [8]

CHAPTER 15

Dealing with People

DEALING with people is perhaps the hardest operation in wildlife management. It requires educating the public in wildlife conservation and in humaneness, advising legislators and courts of law, enforcing game laws, calming irate farmers whose crops have been damaged by wildlife, arranging for access to private lands, and training conservation workers. A Pennslyvania game warden said recently that the biggest change he had seen in twenty-eight years of service was that he now spends more time with people than with animals.

Who are the modern educators in wildlife management? What new theories are shaping its course? The old pros will answer that management has no great need of improvement. It is firmly based on sound, sensible, scientific principles, and if it is under attack by a few persons (like myself) whom it calls "moralist protectionists," this is because management has failed to deliver its message. Its information-and-education department has fallen down on the job. The new conservationists will answer that management has buried its nose in technology, has lost its grasp of the human activities which sustain wildlife, and is trying to justify itself.

Twenty years ago, while I was dealing with forest and range wildlife in Colorado, I proposed to colleagues that we draft a creed, or statement of principles, policies, and practices in wildlife management. Looking back, the proposal seems naive. I see now that people shy away from policies, and when they can actually agree upon one, it is apt to come shapeless from the delivery room. The Wildlife Society did eventually draft a code of ethics which, in the 1971 version, reads: "Members . . . have a responsibility for contributing to an understanding of man's proper relationship with natural resources, and, in particular, for determining the role of wildlife in satisfying human needs." [1]

HUNDREDS of American organizations offer education in wildlife values. They try to explain the complex interplay between wild animals and civilized people. Although each one has its own program and its own bias, I believe that the aims of the organizations can be divided into two main groups, one more utilitarian and the other more humanitarian.

Distinctly utilitarian in their aims, and foremost in

the field of wildlife education, are the game departments of the fifty states. These issue thousands of magazines, special booklets on management, colored bird-and-mammal charts for schools, and other literature that reaches 14 million hunters and their families. Game department employees enter into school and community programs, appear on television, create departmental movies, work with youth groups, train hunters, and put on field demonstrations ("show-me trips") for community leaders.

Major sources of conservation information for sportsmen are the outdoor magazines, especially *Field and Stream, Outdoor Life,* and *Sports Afield.* A study by a graduate in environmental journalism reports that these three periodicals jumped their coverage of environmental information nearly one-third between 1968 and 1970.[2] The outdoor magazines depend on the game departments for a great deal of news on hunting and fishing, and they tend to support the programs of the departments.

Next in influence, I believe, are the national wildlife organizations—membership-supported, nonprofit, educationally oriented, deeply involved in saving wildlife habitats, and ideologically comfortable with killing for sport and commerce. The largest, the National Wildlife Federation, publishes the handsome *National Wildlife Magazine, Ranger Rick's Nature Magazine* for children, *Conservation News, Conservation Report* (while Congress is in session), the valuable *Conservation Directory,* and assorted pamphlets, wildlife stamps, and albums.

The Federation is concerned with saving outdoor

environments for wildlife and for people. Since 1969 it has published periodically an index of environmental quality—which it calls a "National EQ"—as a baseline from which to measure changes upward or downward.[3] Using all the numerical data it can gather, along with opinions sampled by the Gallup Organization, it rates American air, water, soil, forests, wildlife, minerals, and living space on a scale where 100 is ideal. The four indexes published to date suggest a decline: 1969, poor [no numerical rating], 1970, 57.0; 1971, 55.5; and 1973, 54.4. The Federation's effort is worthwhile for its dramatic educational value and for the fact that it tells the ordinary citizen how he can apply pressure against the corporate degraders of the American environment.

The Wildlife Management Institute sponsors the annual North American Wildlife and Natural Resources Conference, a series launched by President Franklin D. Roosevelt in 1936. Young wildlife managers cut their professional teeth by giving a paper at "the Conference."

The World Wildlife Fund has an American office in Washington, D. C., and is affiliated with the International Union for the Conservation of Nature and Natural Resources. The aim of the Fund is to support the conservation of nature by publicity, by education, and by raising funds and allocating them to projects. The activities of the Fund take up 300 pages of description in its most recent yearbook.

The gun and ammunition manufacturing firm Winchester-Western, a division of Olin Corporation, has a conservation department which publishes booklets on wildlife.[4] Not surprisingly, these stress the importance of shooting "surplus" populations of birds and mammals. The Standard Oil Company of California publishes a guide for teachers which claims that "the best friends of our wildlife may well be our sportsmen."[5]

≽

AMONG the humanitarian organizations are the natural-history clubs and the humane societies—nonprofit, membership-supported, either uninterested in or opposed to the killing of wild animals in sport and commerce. (These are called "militant groups" by the same persons who label enemy troops in war as "terrorists.") The purpose of the National Audubon Society, founded in 1905, is to promote the conservation of wildlife and the natural environment, and to educate men, women, and children regarding their place within that environment. *Audubon,* the journal of the society, is one of the most striking pictorial magazines in the world. Many American communities are turning to the Society for help through its guidebooks on nature centers, nature trails, and habitat improvement.

Defenders of Wildlife, incorporated in 1949 and bolstered by a bequest from Rachel Carson, promotes, through education and research, the protection and humane treatment of all wildlife and the elimination of painful methods of trapping, capturing, and killing wildlife. Its quarterly *News* contains the latest bulletins from the battlefront in the war to save habitats. Some of the local humane societies federated in the American Humane Association (founded in 1877) have brought action to ban shooting of tethered live animals, hunting with bows and arrows, hunting with antiquated rifles, and hunting from aircraft.

There is not, to my knowledge, any North American group for which the name "Wildlife Education Association" would be appropriate. In theory, this would be an organization of professional educators in biology and the humanities, devoted to the development of skills, methods, and programs in wildlife education. It would be influential at all educational levels. It would search for truth (I don't say it would find it). It would denounce fakery, special-interest bias, and sloppy sentimentalism in the portrayal of wildlife behavior.

Several groups devoted to broad aspects of education for conservation of natural resources, including wildlife, do exist. The Conservation Education Association (founded in 1953), the Committee for Environmental Information (1958), and the Association of Interpretive Naturalists (1961) are among them.

The aim of the League of Conservation Voters (1970) is education with political action. The League rates congressmen and senators according to the way they voted on key environmental issues. If a legislator voted right by League standards on each of fifteen to twenty selected issues, he is scored 100. In 1971, Senator

William Proxmire of Wisconsin, noted for his conservation zeal, scored 94; Congresswoman Bella S. Abzug of New York was among fourteen who scored 93, the highest attained by anyone in the House that year.[6] By releasing its voting charts to the news media in advance of upcoming elections, the League takes an open stand as a lobbyist for clean environments, free-running streams, preserves, and other advantages for wildlife. If the individual is going to make a difference in future legislation for wildlife, I see promise in the sort of pressure group which the League exemplifies.

On a November evening in 1969, about 24 million television viewers saw a Metro-Goldwyn-Mayer documentary entitled "The Wolf Men." It was intended to create compassion for the few wolves remaining in North America, and it was successful. A great spontaneous outpouring of letters came from the public—6,000 addressed to the Bureau of Sport Fisheries and Wildlife, 5,000 to the Governor of Alaska, and 5,000 to Metro-Goldwyn-Mayer. Three weeks after the showing of the film, bills were introduced in Congress which led to an act banning the shooting of wildlife from aircraft.[7]

WILDLIFE management is routinely involved with the enforcement of game regulations. Beyond this chore is its larger role in guiding the evolution of wildlife law itself. Certain legal issues with respect to wildlife are continually moot. Is hunting on public land an American right or a privilege? Should a citizen who does not buy a hunting license have a voice in the drafting of hunting regulations? What are the most useful roles of state and federal governments, respectively, in wildlife management? Should a state charge out-of-state hunters more than its own residents for the privilege of hunting on federal land? Should governments use the power of eminent domain to acquire key areas for wildlife survival? Is the state or the federal government responsible for wildlife research on federal lands? Should livestock owners who use federal grazing land be permitted to block public access to such land?

The legal aspects of America's national lands were touched upon by the Public Land Law Review Commission's report of 1970 and by an independent review of the report published in the same year.[8]

The Conservation Law Society of America (founded in 1964) provides legal talent to assist conservation groups in their struggle to save wild environments from abuse. It helped save Bolinas Lagoon, California, a waterfowl sanctuary, from exploitation. It is waging a tough fight against the enormously wealthy Walt Disney Enterprises which plan to commercialize Mineral King Valley, California, a game refuge in the midst of a national forest. Perhaps the most useful of the society's activities is its counsel to the environmental law societies now sprouting on college campuses over the nation.

The state game departments have historically paid

no attention to the legal "rights" of the animal itself, as witness the fact that most of them condone—if not promote—the use of cruel devices in trapping (the leg-hold trap), in hunting (the bow and arrow), and in predator control (nonselective poisons). The Animal Welfare Institute (founded in 1951), along with other humane societies, is trying to correct this imbalance; it insists that dealing with the rights of animals is an essential part of wildlife management. The Institute has published a book which summarizes the evolution in America of the concept of animal rights.[9]

Now and then, wild animals inflict damage upon crops or livestock or to game populations valuable in sport under circumstances in which control of the nuisance animals appears to be too expensive. Wildlife managers may then simply arrange to pay off the injured parties in cash. The operation is called mitigation. It is redemptive, rather than preventive, though within the American system it is an acceptable way of dealing with a people-wildlife impasse.

Mitigation is employed mainly in water development projects. Many years ago, the City of Seattle built a dam on the Skagit River for electric power. Now the city wants to raise the dam, pushing a reservoir into Canada and flooding the wild and beautiful Big Beaver Valley. Conservationists have temporarily halted the proj-

ects, and meanwhile the Washington State Game Department is thinking about ways of cushioning the impact if the dam should eventually be raised. Seattle
might, for example, pay the department a flat sum. The
department would not take the money as heart balm; it
would spend it to improve habitats for game animals and
furbearers elsewhere in Washington.

But what is the value of a cedar valley a million
years in the making? How does one "buy" a living deer,
or a beaver, or a sooty grouse? The Washington Game
Department is already receiving about $400,000 a year
from other agencies in compensation for loss of wildlife
habitat. These dollars have little more meaning than
those paid to a miner's widow for loss of a human life.

The policy of the Wildlife Society is "to oppose
publicly funded stream alteration programs . . . until
replacement in kind of fish and wildlife habitat is included in project cost calculations and authorization re-
quests." [10]

President Nixon vetoed an act which would have
compensated the people of Montana for destruction of
wildlife habitat caused by the Army Corps of Engineers'
Libby Dam Project. As I write in 1973, the waters are
flooding 28,000 acres of brush-covered river bottom, a
critical winter range for deer and elk.

The idea of depredation insurance, or insurance
against unusual damage to crops or livestock from the
harmful food habits of wild animals, is under study. It
could be one approach to alleviation of damage. Insur-

ance companies have not been attracted to wildlife risk because estimates of damages tend to be imprecise or biased. A sheepman who complains about the awful impact of eagles upon his lambs may be able to convince his friendly congressman but not his insurance broker.

The Province of Saskatchewan, finding that no private insurance companies were interested, began in 1953 to insure farmers against crop losses from ducks, geese, sandhill cranes, deer, elk, antelope, and bear. For a 2-percent premium, the government offers maximum coverage of $25 per acre. Through 1971, on a yearly average, 553 farmers collectively paid $29,000 in premiums and received $146,000 in insurance claims.[11] The Province made up the difference by dipping into the sporting license fund. The reasoning was that if a farmer is willing to spare the life of a pheasant eating his sprouted corn, a hunter who later kills that bird should be willing to kick back a few cents to the farmer.

Who is training the wildlife conservationists of tomorrow? Odom Fanning, a Washington-based science writer, estimates that there were 15,000 wildlife "practitioners" in the United States in 1970.[12] As of December 1972, forty-five colleges in North America offered a named degree in wildlife and twenty-seven others offered a wildlife major option with a degree in a related field. In 1971, fifty-nine colleges graduated 1,229 students in some aspect of wildlife management. Within the same year, 29 percent of them obtained wildlife employment, as follows:

	Bachelors	*Masters*	*Doctors*	*All*
Number	179	131	46	356
Percent	20	50	75	29

The 71 percent not placed were identified by the author of the foregoing table as "housewife, unemployed, ill, and deceased." [13]

I believe that training programs which aim to educate in the broadest sense of the word will best serve the profession of wildlife management in the years ahead. The best manager will always be a man or woman who, while appreciating the values of natural outdoor arrangements, enjoys living among other human beings and is concerned about the future of human society.

As long as wildlife training is truthful and exciting, it can, at the earliest levels of schooling, be left with equal assurance to either professionals or amateurs. Wildlife management will be subtly improved if the architectural plans for every new elementary school provide for an outdoor land-for-learning, as well as the traditional sport field or "yard." Every child should be exposed to the laws of nature as well as to the rules of Little League baseball.

PART THREE

AN ETHIC
TOWARD WILDLIFE

CHAPTER 16

The Source of
the Ethic

ABOUT 10 million years ago, the primate stock which was destined to continue on toward mankind was separated by unknown barriers from the stock which was to continue on toward the great apes. About 8 million years later, within that humanoid stock there emerged the tool-storing, value-creating animals called men. It is supposed that early men came to enjoy the company of jungle fowl, goats, sheep, dogs, and cats around their campfires, and it is known that, by 10,000 years ago, men had begun seriously to domesticate, or manage, a half-dozen kinds of birds and mammals. Down to the present time, a few primitive peoples in Africa, Australia, South America, and the Philippines live essentially by hunting and fishing, grubbing for roots, and picking seeds and

fruit. This contemporary fact and the evidence of archae-
ology indicate that all peoples, including the "civilized"
ones, have passed through a hunting stage.

Hunting is therefore instinctive, say the modern
sportsmen. It is a natural release for a primal tension that
builds up within a man's blood. (But not within a
woman's. Her chromosomes contain, instead of a gene for
hunting, one for fire tending.) Many sportsmen cannot
understand that *Homo sapiens* is now responsible for his
own evolution and that social heredity, rather than
genetic heredity, will shape his future communities. The
growth of an ethic toward wildlife has resembled the
growth of religions and political structures in the sense
that the results are purely human; none fits any conceiv-
able model of wild-animal evolution.

Nor do many sportsmen seem to realize that man is
the only animal that kills for pleasure. Young wolves will
practice at killing grasshoppers and will seem to enjoy
their play, but that is an exercise in maturation which
cannot be compared to shooting doves with a shotgun
for fun.

"Man has been primarily a hunter during most of
his time on earth," explains the Wildlife Society in a recent policy paper. "Modern sport hunting . . . reenacts
a drama as old as man himself." [1] There is something to
be said for hunting as an art form—a Greek drama in
which all but one of the players are destroyed in the end.

Some argue that, because primitive man had little
sensitivity toward and doubtless no reverence for life

other than his own, modern man should not trouble himself to search for a natural origin of gentleness. That is, if reverence for life is not one of man's genetic endowments, why should he try to defend its essential rightness? But evolution has molded man into a thing unique. He is now more than a superanimal; in his self-awareness he is an altogether different kind of animal. He alone can think of compassion. He alone can look at a living beast in the field without the animal reaction—do I kill it or does it kill me? He alone can afford to wonder about the origin, the meaning, and the end of Life itself.

≥

AT some pastoral or village-industry stage in history near the early Christian era, men began to look at wild animals, not only as parcels of meat, fiber, skin, and bone, but as fellow beings. About then, I think, the corpus of thought identified as the conservation ethic began to divide. From one point of view, the primary value of a natural resource was held to be its contribution to human security-survival, from the other, its contribution to human life-quality. The difference has been described by the biologist René Dubos in a comparison of Franciscan conservation and Benedictine stewardship. To Benedict of Nursia (A.D. 480–543) the meaning of life was work. He intervened actively in natural arrangements of soil, water, and wildlife. Nature to him became relevant at the point where he squeezed its clay between his hands. A humanized landscape was no less beautiful than a wild one. To Francis of Assisi (1182?–1226), the meaning of life was love. He marveled at the "fitness" of wild things out-of-doors; he strove for harmonious equality between man and other organisms. His conservation was mystical, contemplative, and (some would say) escapist. Dubos is able to see the common faith of Francis and Benedict. "Reverence for nature," he concludes, "is compatible with willingness to accept responsibility for a creative stewardship of the earth." [2]

This, I think, is roughly what the new conservationists are saying. The spirit of Francis can be, at the same time, the sustaining energy for and the governor upon wildlife conservation of the future.

CHAPTER 17

The Ethic in Motion

AN ethic toward wildlife is always in motion. It starts with understanding of the mutual needs of people and animals and of the ways in which they harm and benefit one another. That understanding is ecological awareness. Understanding grows into collective attitudes which energize the ethic; it moves faster when educators and persuaders (by whatever name) work harder at changing public taste. The ethic is revealed in action. Men and women of good will toward animals try to establish pyramids of balance in the human uses of wildlife populations. Each pyramid is stratified, and each stratum represents the kind of fauna, rich in variety and numbers, which one particular group of people enjoys or finds useful. In the ideal pyramid, no one use is offensive to persons who favor other uses. As the options in wildlife conservation are acted upon, they reveal new truths and bring new understanding. The ethic comes around in a spiral and it moves.

We Americans need not cherish, simply because it was frontier American, an attitude toward wildlife which is now beginning to trouble the conscience of many thoughtful persons. I venture to predict that the ethic will change in important ways before the end of the twentieth century. The changes will be pushed by persons who are disturbed by the failure of older generations to conserve wildlife habitats and wildlife diversity and by the killing of wild birds and mammals today for sport and commerce. Many of these persons are not very articulate, and they are not experts in biology or wildlife management. They are plain people who question the American ethic toward the wolf. They feel intuitively that the fate of the wolf and the fate of man are the same.

These people, whom I have called the new conservationists, are at a moral frontier. They are propelled by a concern which keeps them headed toward a decent society, a society that seems to them not only "right" but natural and sensible. The sportsman and the fur trapper will complain that the new conservationists—referred to by them as deep-breathers, weepers, bleeding hearts, idealists, or posy sniffers—are mixing "emotion" with "fact," to the confusion of the voting public which cannot distinguish one from the other. But should one try to pull emotion apart from fact? "Knowledge without feeling," says the poet Archibald MacLeish, "is not knowledge." [1]

The Ethic in Motion

≽

THE changes that I venture to predict in the American ethic toward wildlife are of two kinds: practical improvements in wildlife management that seem both necessary and feasible (the question of how) and the development of a new rationale for management itself (the question of why). The two approaches are reflected in the questions put earlier about the clubbing of seals for the fur trade: Is there a better way to kill a seal and should seals be killed at all? Let me begin with the changes in practices that I anticipate.

Wildlife management will achieve a more democratic base.

The state agency responsible for conserving the people's wildlife will no longer be called the game department but the wildlife department, or an equivalent. Its policy-making officers will include not only sportsmen, farmers, livestock ranchers, and businessmen, but representatives of conservation organizations such as the Wilderness Society, of humane societies such as the Animal Welfare Institute, and of civic-action groups such as the League of Conservation Voters. They will include many more women; today, 99 percent of the members of game commissions are men.

As it moves to a broader base, wildlife management

will be financed more out of tax revenues and less out of hunting and trapping licenses. There is already some visible motion in this direction. The new move toward broad-base financing will be strongly resisted, because game departments value their autonomy and sportsmen like to say, "We saved the wildlife and we support it." There is danger that they will slip into the habit of saying, "It is *our* wildlife and *our* wild countryside."

Wherever the ties between a wildlife department and a clientele group threaten to pull conservation off its democratic base, those ties will be loosened. At present, undue influence is brought to bear upon game departments by manufacturers of sporting goods and by special-interest groups which emphasize varmint hunting and trophy hunting. Clientele support is not always wrong, but it is always dangerous.

A case in point is the influence of the American gun business, which sold more than half a billion dollars' worth of firearms and supplies in 1972. The barrage of propaganda put out by that business is surely responsible in part for the posture of the Wildlife Society, which claims that "restrictive measures which discourage the American hunter's pursuit of his sport will . . . curtail wildlife conservation and management programs." It therefore "opposes legislation that impedes or prohibits the legitimate use or acquisition of sporting arms and ammunition." [2] This attitude does not admit the probability that law enforcement in the United States would be simpler and better if the mere possession of an unregistered gun were *de jure* evidence of criminal intent.

An official of the National Shooting Sports Foundation has recently shown, with the help of statistics, that crime rates are highest in those states where the per capita sales of hunting licenses are lowest. This means, he claims, that crime is linked with a scarcity of firearms.[3] But surely the real link is with geography. Crime is lowest in hunting regions and highest in urbanized, industrialized regions where few hunting licenses are sold.

State and federal wildlife agencies will cater more and more to persons who wish to use wild animals in appreciative, nonconsumptive ways.

These are the people who like to watch and listen to living birds and mammals out of doors and to let them live. These are the people who see values in deer and fur seals other than their values as living targets or crops.

"Wildlife conservation must be practiced not only for the consumer, the sportsman—generally thought of as the hunter—but also for the ever-increasing proportion of people who simply enjoy seeing and hearing wild animals in their native habitat, or for that matter, simply enjoy the knowledge that these animals do exist. We are more cognizant than ever of the esthetic value of our total wildlife resource."[4]

These words come from the director of a federal agency whose men killed over a million coyotes, bobcats, bears, wolves, and cougars during the 1960s; an agency which still allows state game departments to dictate hunting policy on federal lands. Yet even within that agency some are listening to the faint rustlings of a changing wind.

American wildlife management originated in game management; its technology stems from the ideas of Aldo Leopold, Ira Gabrielson, and their colleagues in the 1930s. Those men were naturalists and hunters. It would be unfair and untrue to say that, because they were hunters, they were set against nature. Even today, many hunters inherit the hunting faith along with the family religion and only later in life, through conversion, become also conservationists and naturalists.

But different ages need different impulses. Americans are newly aware of the values of game animals alive and are seeing new values in the so-called non-game species. Between 1960 and 1970, membership in the National Audubon Society rose from 32,000 to 121,000 and membership in the Defenders of Wildlife from 3,500 to 22,000, while the number of sport-hunters either declined or increased only slightly, depending on whose data one accepts. In the *New York Times* in 1973, Marylin Bender reported that "of the gun manufacturers polled, 67.4 percent said they thought hunting and shooting would become less important in the next five years, the most pessimistic forecast for any recreational activity." [5] The predicted change in public attitude toward hunting will, I think, parallel the change that often takes place in the philosophy of an old hunter as he grows more perceptive of his place among other forms of life.

The future will see a rise in the number of high-quality beast parks, photographic safaris to bird islands, visits to whale-watching observatories, and other spectaculars which will aim to develop rapport between people and wildlife. This field of education has been little explored; it methodology will have to improve. Its critical problem at the moment is how to maintain naturalness in situations where visitors are intruders.

Market hunting will come to an end; sport-hunting will continue in cleaner, more humane, and more imaginative ways.

By market hunting I mean the trapping and clubbing of furbearers, the shooting of animals for the pet-food industry, the live-capturing of rabbits for coursing, the capturing of hawks for sale to falconers, and similar pursuits of wild birds and mammals for commercial ends. The Friends of the Earth organization (founded in 1969) has already taken the position that the use of wild animal products as objects of commerce should be discouraged.

In sport-hunting of the future, mechanical devices which come between the living man and his living prey—the gadgets that insulate the hunter in body and spirit from the hunted—will decline in favor. The whole quality, or drama, if you wish, of the outdoor hunting experience will be stressed, while the animal yield—the number of ducks, the number of points on the elk rack, the number of feet collected in the crow-shooting contest—will be played down. The hunter will hunt because of the activity itself, not for its effects. He will look for new ways to handicap himself, though not at the expense of humaneness to the animal.

Populations of certain native game species will be stimulated through improvement of habitats. The deliberate importation of exotic species will be banned. The renewal of native species in habitats which they or closely related species once occupied will be encouraged.

Sport-shooters will increasingly depend upon game birds raised within private shooting grounds. The Wildlife Society recommends that such grounds remain in private hands; public agencies should get out of the act and stay out.

Deliberate improvement of habitats for those big-game species which tend to become destructive will be discouraged. In the past, by means of predatory-animal control, supplementary feeding, and manipulation of vegetative cover, high populations of deer and elk have been routinely encouraged. These practices often lead to crowding of animals and abuse of vegetation, whereupon the hunters cry: "Overpopulation! Extend the hunting season!" In the midst of a deer irruption, the land manager ought to ask himself to what extent man, the newcomer and intruder, is responsible for the imbalance.

Shooters will substitute moving inanimate targets— clay birds and the like—for live birds and mammals in archery and gunnery fun. The baiting for sport of tethered birds and mammals, such as turkeys and raccoons, will disappear in the very near future. Sportsmen will abandon the bow and arrow and the muzzle-loader, though reluctantly, for they insist that these toys add zest to hunting and are not demonstrably more cruel than a high-powered rifle or shotgun.

Federal intervention to raise the standards of hunting will increase as a result of citizen pressure. The government has already moved, in legal areas where it has undisputed jurisdiction, to correct abuses in the hunting of migratory birds, marine mammals, and endangered species. As one striking example, whaling by Americans was brought to an end in 1972. Whales had been killed by bombs, a method more cruel than any practiced in a slaughterhouse. As the United States of America nears its two-hundredth birthday, it is fitting that the nation should raise legal barriers against cruelty toward wild animals, as it has already raised them against cruelty toward domestic animals, pets, and children.

Research into new methods of controlling nuisance populations of animals will receive a substantial share of the moneys now poured into poisoning, shooting, and trapping of those animals.

Future control will start with restrictions on importations of potentially dangerous species. It will depend on mechanical protection (for example, fences and moats), use of sheep dogs and herders, repellents (bad-tasting or bad-smelling chemicals, annoying sights and sounds), environmental controls (biocontrols), and, as a last resort, transfer or direct killing of nuisance individuals.

The Ethic in Motion

Wildlife on national lands will increasingly be managed as a national resource.

The 700 million acres of federal land are a treasure-house of wildlife. An American ethic toward wildlife is bound to consider principles of right conduct toward the people's birds and mammals living on the people's land. I predict that the government will act more and more like a genuine trustee, or steward, of its wildlife environments. Fuzzy legal interpretations of federal as against local responsibility for land-use decisions affecting wildlife will be clarified. Class action suits brought by the Environmental Defense Fund and similar groups will push the federal government into truly all-American decisions, as compared with decisions in favor of local sheepowners, sport hunters, and trappers. (The Environmental Defense Fund, founded in 1967, is a national, nonprofit organization of lawyers and scientists which serves as the legal action arm for the scientific community.)

The term multiple use with respect to wildlife on public lands will be redefined to apply only to the pyramid of uses which is practical in regions of vast size or diverse habitats. Within the pyramid, dominant, or single, or special uses will be stratified. On some lands, not all the potential uses will be permitted. No estuary in America can stand up under simultaneous demands for transportation, waste disposal, generation of tidal power, fishing, sailing, boat building, oil refining, and wildlife production, or more than a fraction of these demands. Too many estuaries have already been ruined by thoughtless or ignorant popular pressure for all things for all people in all places.

In the pyramid of uses of wildlife on public lands, the lowest and the highest strata will have characteristics somewhat as follows:

Lowest stratum: Popular; on land near urban centers, small, somewhat artificial and mechanized, often noisy, for day use. Examples: bird-and-beast watching, crow shooting at Fort Cobb, Oklahoma, and duck hunting on many state and national waterfowl marshes.

Highest stratum: Attractive to a few specialists; on land remote and scenic, vast, primitive, natural, without mechanized transportation, quiet, for vacation use, or for study sessions of a week or longer. Examples: "one-shot" animal hunting; supervised visits to heron rookeries and seal islands; attending "wolf howls" in national parks; studying grizzly-bear ecology in Montana wilderness.

Before establishing pyramids of use, emphasis will be placed on biological and demographic surveys—studies of the distribution, variation, and numbers of birds and mammals and studies of the distribution, numbers, and interests of people. Land-use classification and planning will follow.

As a final prediction of change, I suggest that the wildlife management process will increasingly open itself to examination. Its aims and methods will be debated more freely and honestly than in the past. News releases from the local wildlife agency will be sent not only to "outdoor writers" (a curious term) but to the local officers of humane societies and garden clubs. Meetings of wildlife commissions will be open to the press. Citizen advisory groups will help government wildlife agencies to resolve conflict-of-use arguments involving public attitudes and preferences.

≥

In predicting changes in the basic philosophy of wildlife management, I face the question: What are the rights of an animal in relation to the rights of man? As a biologist, I believe that, where one must be sacrificed for the other, the animal has to go. Though man, too, is an animal, he is the only one for which important further evolution is open. He is the only one that can sense the richness of life. He is the only one that can plan, and therefore the only one that can take action to preserve that richness.

The concept of wildlife as a common good is difficult to grasp. I have a legal share—a proprietary right—in every wild bird and mammal in my home state of Washington and, to a degree, in the whole United States. I have a moral share in every living thing on earth, wild or tame. We are all caught up together in a sort of sensible biomass. All pain is our own pain. When a raccoon breaks its leg and crushes its teeth in a steel trap, the fur trapper may defend his legal right to inflict that harm but he cannot defend his right to damage my moral interest. He may argue that ideals are a luxury which he, a poor trapper, cannot afford—he makes his living by being practical. I reply that he will have to find some other occupation which will not hurt me through the pain and terror of raccoons.

Stuart Hampshire, Warden of Wadham College, Oxford, England, wonders about morality within conservation. He asks: "May the natural order be farmed [compare hunted and trapped] by human beings for their comfort and pleasure without any restriction other than the comfort and pleasure of future human beings?" He answers himself that "the natural order as a whole is the fitting object of that kind of unconditional interest and respect that is called moral." If there are no countervailing reasons for rejecting a way of life—a set of actions—its felt and historically proven "naturalness" is a reason for accepting it. "The exceptional value attached both to individual lives, and to the survival of the species as a whole, resides in the power of the human mind to begin to understand, and to enjoy, the natural order as a whole." [6]

I would carry the argument further. The killing of a wild animal is moral in so far as it satisfies a human need, is accomplished in a natural manner, and leaves the natural community of the animal undisturbed. In the future, the priorities of killing wild animals will be in descending order: for subsistence; for protection against certain animal habits and against diseases which animals carry; for sport; and for vanity.

⟩

THERE is a parameter called poetically "the resonance of the world"—a measure of the slow vibration of earth. The new conservationists are trying to synchronize the plans of men with that vibration, as though it were the pulse of a great mother organism. Their efforts are difficult in a time of crumbling cities and stinking rivers, destructive wars, and gasoline engines as thick as lice, but the goal is none the less the only one that has meaning.

For the new conservationists, the old theologies do not work and the rulebooks are seen to offer quaint advice. The slogans of earlier teachers with respect to wildlife—"conservation through use," "preservation of species through cropping," and "maximum sustainable yield of the wildlife resource"—are seen to be, not wrong, but incomplete. They lack humanity. They fail to include the effect of killing upon the feelings of people.

People hunger for reassurance; they would like to think that humankind is moving upward. The new conservationists are saying: To the degree that we can learn to live with our wild brethren without wanting to kill them, we will reinforce an inner belief (which can never be proved) that life itself has meaning and purpose and direction.

REFERENCE NOTES

FOR FURTHER READING

INDEX

❧ *Reference Notes*

INTRODUCTION

1. Patrick Corbett, "Postscript," in *Animals, Men and Morals,* ed. Stanley and Roslind Godlovich and John Harris (London: Victor Gollancz, 1971), p. 236.

2. "What Happened at Stockholm—a Special Report," *Science and Public Affairs* 28, no. 7 (1972): 16, 33.

3. Carl Sagan, Linda Salzman Sagan, and Frank Drake, "A Message from Earth," *Science* 175 (1972): 881–884.

4. Arlen J. Large, "Opposition Vanishes as Some Kids Gang Up to Save Wild Horses," *Wall Street Journal,* April 19, 1971, p. 1.

5. Loren Eiseley, "Magic," *Notes of an Alchemist* (New York: Charles Scribner's Sons, 1972), p. 65.

6. George R. Hall, "Conservation as a Public Policy Goal," *Yale Review* 51, no. 3 (1962): 413.

7. Isaac Asimov, "At Stake: 500,000,000 Years of Life," *National Wildlife* 10, no. 3 (1972): 4–13.

8. Ernest P. Walker, *Animal Behavior,* Smithsonian Report for 1940 (Washington, D.C., 1941), p. 312.

9. Reuben Edwin Trippensee, *Wildlife Management* (New York: McGraw-Hill, American Forestry Series, 1948).

10. Yochelson, Ellis L., "Man's Rights over Nature," *Science* 166 (1969): 1576.

1. SHOOTING FOR SPORT

1. U.S. Bureau of Sport Fisheries and Wildlife, *1970 Survey of Fishing and Hunting*, Resource Publication 95 (1972).

2. U.S. Bureau of Sport Fisheries and Wildlife, *1960 National Survey of Fishing and Hunting*, Circular 120 (1961).

3. U.S. Bureau of Sport Fisheries and Wildlife, Fact Sheets with letter to the author from Willis King, assistant director, January 22, 1973, on hunting license sales 1960–1970.

4. Marilyn Bender, "The Gun Business on the Defensive," *New York Times*, March 4, 1973, sec. 3:1, 9.

5. Joseph P. Linduska, "Hunting Is a Positive Thing" in *Birds in Our Lives*, ed. Alfred Stefferud (New York: Arco, 1970), p. 111; U.S. Bureau of Sport Fisheries and Wildlife, *Waterfowl Harvest and Hunter Activity in the United States during the 1971 Hunting Season*, Administrative Report no. 216 (Laurel, Md., 1972); and *Big Game Inventory for 1970*, Wildlife Leaflet 497 (1971).

6. Edward A. McLarney, "Family Plan Hunting," *American Rifleman* 120, no. 9 (1972): 26–28.

7. Thomas Gilbert Pearson, *Adventures in Bird Protection* (New York: Appleton-Century, 1937), pp. 231–234.

8. Prince Philip (Duke of Edinburgh) and James Fisher, *Wildlife Crisis* (New York: Cowles Co. and World Wildlife Fund, 1970), p. 26.

9. Brad O'Connor, "At Last, Day for Sportsmen!" *Seattle Times*, September 21, 1972, D–9.

10. Ben East, "The Big Lie," *Outdoor Life*, June, July, and August, 1972; available as reprint, 22 pp.

11. Robert Franklin Leslie, *The Bears and I: Raising Three Cubs in the North Woods* (New York: Ballantine, 1971), p. 184.

12. National Audubon Society, "Hunters and Conservationists Share Goals," *National Wildlife* 9, no. 6 (1971): 18.

13. American Humane Association, *Position Statement on Sport Hunting* (Denver, Colo., 1973).

14. A. Starker Leopold, "The Essence of Hunting," *National Wildlife* 10, no. 6 (1972): 38–40.

15. Daniel A. Poole, "Insuring the Future of Hunting and Fishing," *Wildlife Society News,* no. 136 (1971): 45–46.

16. Russell E. Train, "Big Game Hunting and the Environmental Age," in *North American Big Game* (Pittsburgh: Boone and Crockett Club, 1971), p. 96.

2. ODD WAYS OF HUNTING

1. Letter to the author, November 24, 1972.

2. Keith C. Schuyler, "Trophy and the Triumph," *Pennsylvania Game News* 43, no. 11 (1972): 58.

3. Winchester-Western, "North American Shooting Preserve Directory 1972–73," 12-page insert in *Outdoor Life* 150, no. 4 (1972).

4. Jack Samson, "The One-Shot Antelope Hunt," *Field and Stream* 77, no. 9 (1973): 107.

5. *North American Big Game* (Pittsburgh: Boone and Crockett Club, 1971), p. ix.

6. W. Leslie Robinette, *Deer Mortality from Gunshot Wounds,* U.S. Fish and Wildlife Service Wildlife Leaflet 295 (1947), pp. 5, 7.

7. Jack O'Connor, "The Grand Slam Caper," *Outdoor Life* 151, no. 1 (1973): 156.

8. John Steinbeck and Edward F. Ricketts, *Sea of Cortez: A Leisurely Journal of Travel and Research* (New York: Viking, 1941), pp. 163–167.

9. Public Law 92–159.

10. Jim Hunter, "Aerial Hunting of Wildlife . . . Violates Existing Federal Aviation Administration Regulations," *Defenders of Wildlife News* 47, no. 5 (1972): 508.

11. Larry Kruckenberg, "The Red Fox and Coyote in North Da-

kota. Part 2. The Red Fox," *North Dakota Outdoors* 34, no. 4 (1971): 17.

12. U.S. State Department, *Additions to Conference between United States and United Mexican States for Protection of Migratory Birds and Game Mammals* (Mexico City, March 10, 1972). This amends the Migratory Bird Treaty Act of 1936 (16 U.S. Code 703–711).

13. Grove Pet Ranch, *Pets from the Four Corners of the World* (Hialeah Lakes, Fla., 1973), p. 3.

3. KILLING FOR SUBSISTENCE

1. Charles D. Brower, *Fifty Years Below Zero* (New York: Dodd, Mead, 1942); Vilhjalmur Stefansson, *My Life with the Eskimo* (New York: Macmillan, 1919).

2. Richard K. Nelson, *Hunters of the Northern Ice* (Chicago: University of Chicago Press, 1969), p. 194.

3. Public Law 92–522.

4. Aldo Leopold, *A Sand County Almanac* (New York: Oxford University Press, 1949), p. 207; Charles Elton, *The Ecology of Invasion by Animals and Plants* (London: Methuen, 1958), p. 145.

5. George Catlin, *North American Indians . . . 1832–1839* (Edinburgh: John Grant, 1926), 1:288–289.

6. American Friends Service Committee, *Uncommon Controversy* (Seattle: University of Washington Press, 1970), back cover.

4. KILLING FOR THE FUR TRADE

1. U.S. Bureau of Domestic Commerce, tables on fur imports and exports, 1965–71; given in letter to author, October 24, 1972;

Reference Notes

U.S. Bureau of Sport Fisheries and Wildlife, *Fur Catch in the United States, 1970,* Wildlife Leaflet 499 (1971); U.S. Statistical Reporting Service, "*Mink Production* [in U.S., 1971]," Department of Agriculture news release, June 5, 1972.

2. Christopher M. Korth, Thomas N. Gladwin, and Ruediger Naumann-Etienne, *U.S. Mink Ranching in World Markets* (Ann Arbor, Mich.: University of Michigan Institute for International Commerce), p. 61.

3. Fur Information and Fashion Council, quoted in Cathy Lerza, "The Fur Industry: an Endangered Species?" *Environmental Action* 4, 15 (1972): 3.

4. "The Furriers Wear a Hunted Look," *Business Week* 2203 (November 20, 1971): 42.

5. "A Furrier's Credo," *Fur Age Weekly,* June 7, 1971, p. 8.

6. Fur Takers of America, *Constitution* (Mehlville, Mo., 1972), p. 1.

7. U.S. Bureau of Sport Fisheries and Wildlife, *Threatened Wildlife of the United States,* Resource Publication 114 (Washington, D.C., 1973), p. 289.

8. "Protest, Priorities, and the Alaska Fur Seal," *Audubon* 72, no. 2 (1970): 114–115.

9. Quoted in *New York Times Book Review,* October 22, 1972, p. 32.

10. U.S. Senate, Committee on Commerce, *Ocean Mammal Protection, Hearings,* 92d Cong., 2d. sess. 1972, serial no. 92–56, 470.

11. T. S. Eliot, "Burnt Norton," *Four Quartets* (New York: Harcourt, Brace & World, 1943), p. 4.

12. Robert W. Rand, "Conservation of Cape Fur Seals," Lecture to Wildlife Society, Transvaal Branch, Johannesburg, South Africa, November 7, 1972.

13. "Beware Visitors!" (editorial), *Fur Trade Journal* (Bewdley, Ont.) 50, 9 (1972): 3.

14. Stewart M. Brandborg, *A Handbook on the Wilderness Act* (Washington, D.C.: Wilderness Society, 1970).

15. Richard M. Nixon, "Environmental Safeguards on Activities for Animal Damage Control on Federal Lands," Executive Order 11643, February 8, 1972 (FR Doc. 72-2032).

16. E. F. Timme and Son (New York), letter to author, June 26, 1972, with ads for fake furs.

17. Mary Hamman, "Conservation Ruffles Fur in Fashion World," *Smithsonian* 1, no. 6 (1970): 54–55.

18. Abe Feinglass, "We Need to Draw Together," *Fur Age Weekly* 99, no. 20 (1971): 2.

19. Donald Baillie, quoted in F. Jean Vintner, *Facts about Furs* (London: Universities Federation for Animal Welfare, 1957), p. 3.

20. U.S. Congress, House, A Bill to Discourage the Use of Leg-Hold or Steel Jaw Traps on Animals in the United States, H.R. 8784, introduced by William S. Broomfield, Representative, Michigan, June 1, 1971.

21. International Union for the Conservation of Nature and Natural Resources, *IUCN/WWF Concern with the Fur Industry* (Morges, Switzerland, 1972).

5. KILLING FOR SCIENCE

1. Charles Miller Harris, "A Cruise after Sea Elephants," *Pacific Monthly* 21, no. 4 (1909): 336.

2. Sydney Anderson, J. Kenneth Doutt, and James S. Findley, "Collections of Mammals in North America," *Journal of Mammalogy* 44, no. 4 (1963): 471–500; Richard C. Banks, Mary H. Clench, and Jon C. Barlow, "Bird Collections in the United States and Canada," *Auk*, 90 no. 1 (1973): 136–170.

3. Thomas Gilbert Pearson, *Adventures in Bird Protection* (New York: D. Appleton-Century, 1937), p. 217.

4. Donald A. Dayton, Superintendent, Carlsbad Caverns National Park, in letter to the author, April 4, 1973.

5. Walter W. Dalquest, *Mammals of Washington,* University of Kansas, Museum of Natural History Publications, vol. 2. (Lawrence, Kans., 1948).

Reference Notes

6. Arnold Small, "A Word on Behalf of the Rare Bird," *Western Tanager* (Los Angeles) 38, no. 1 (1971): 1.

7. John Fowles, "The Blinded Eye," *Animals* (London) 13, no. 9 (1971): 392.

6. SEALING: A THREAT TO THE ANTARCTIC?

1. Albert W. Erickson, Wilderness Research Center, University of Idaho, Moscow, to the author, November 8, 1972.

2. James E. Heg, "Conference on the Conservation of Antarctic Seals," *Antarctic Journal of the United States* 7, no. 3 (1972): 45–49. *Report of the Conference on the Conservation of Antarctic Seals* (London: Foreign and Commonwealth Office, 1972).

3. U.S. State Department, "Convention for the Conservation of Antarctic Seals," press release no. 44 (February 17, 1972), p. 1.

4. Letter from Per Martens, G. C. Rieber & Co., Bergen, Norway, to the author, November 28, 1972.

5. National Audubon Society, New York Zoological Society, and Defenders of Wildlife (signatories), to U.S. Secretary of State, February 10, 1972.

6. Cleveland Amory, "The Rape of a Continent," *Fund for Animals* (New York), June 1972, 1; "Antarctic Sanctuary No Longer?" *New York Times,* February 6, 1972, sec. 4:12; U.S. National Park Service (primary sponsor), "Recommendations Adopted at the Final Conference Session, September 27, 1972, at Grand Teton National Park, Wyoming, U.S.A.," *Second World Conference on National Parks* (Washington, D.C., 1972), p. 5.

7. Nigel Sitwell, "Sealing in the Antarctic," *Animals* (London) 14, no. 4 (1972): 147.

8. Nigel Sitwell, "Comment" [on Antarctic sealing], *Humane Society of the United States News,* Summer, 1972, p. 5.

9. Brian Roberts, Polar Regions Section, Latin America Depart-

ment, Foreign and Commonwealth Department, United Kingdom, letters to the author, December 6, 1972, and March 16, 1973.

7. SHUFFLING WILDLIFE FAUNAS

1. Roy Bongartz, "Why Not Try a Hunting Vacation in Texas? You Can't Miss," *New York Times,* April 1, 1973, sec. 10:1, 12.

2. Clyde Jones and John L. Paradiso, *Mammals Imported into the United States in 1969,* U.S. Bureau of Sport Fisheries and Wildlife, Special Scientific Report—Wildlife, no. 147, 1972; Richard C. Banks and Roger B. Clapp, *Birds Imported into the United States in 1969,* U.S. Bureau of Sports Fisheries and Wildlife, Special Scientific Report—Wildlife, no. 148 (1972).

3. U.S. State Department, *Convention on International Trade in Endangered Species of Wild Fauna and Flora* (Washington, D.C., March 3, 1973).

4. Gardiner Bump, "Exotics and the Role of the State-Federal Foreign Game Investigation Program," in Caesar Kleberg Research Program in Wildlife Ecology (Texas A & M University), *Symposium on Introduction of Exotic Animals,* August 27–September 1, 1967 (College Station, Tex., 1968), pp. 5–8.

5. Gardiner Bump, *Foreign Game Investigation; A Federal-State Cooperative Program,* U.S. Bureau of Sport Fisheries and Wildlife, Resource Publication no. 49 (1969), p. 14.

6. "Hunting Preserve Plan Stirs Ire," *Chicago Tribune,* February 22, 1972.

7. Jonas Brothers of Seattle, Washington, brochures and advertisements (1972).

8. Karl W. Kenyon, *The Sea Otter in the Eastern Pacific Ocean,* U.S. Bureau of Sport Fisheries and Wildlife, North American Fauna no. 68 (1969).

9. *Scientific Activities in Fisheries and Wildlife Resources,* Science Council of Canada Special Study no. 15 (Information Canada, Ottawa, 1971), pp. 125–126; A. T. Bergerud, "Newfoundland

Wildlife Management," *Newfoundland Annual Report of the Department of Mines, Agriculture and Resources* (St. John's, 1963), pp. 68–126.

8. GETTING ALONG WITH WILDLIFE

1. Jack Miner, *Jack Miner and the Birds* (Chicago: Reilly and Lee, 1923), p. 24.

2. Edward L. Kozicky and Robert A. McCabe," Birds in Pest Situations," in *Vertebrate Pests: Problems and Control* (Washington, D.C.: National Academy of Sciences, 1970), pp. 58–82.

3. W. Robert Eadie (chairman), "Annual Report of the Committee on Economic Losses Caused by Vertebrates," *Journal of Wildlife Management* 25, no. 3 (1961): 321.

4. Roger Tory Peterson, *Birds over America* (New York: Dodd, Mead, 1964), p. 65.

5. Olsen, Jack, *Slaughter the Animals, Poison the Earth* (New York: Simon & Schuster, 1971).

6. U.S. Bureau of Sport Fisheries and Wildlife, *Sharing the Environment: A Positive Approach to Animal Damage Control* (Washington, D.C.: Government Printing Office, 1968).

7. U.S. Congress, House Committee on Merchant Marine and Fisheries, "Statement of Nathaniel P. Reed, Assistant Secretary for Fish and Wildlife and Parks, Department of the Interior . . ." 92d Cong., 2d sess., 1972, serial no. 92-22, p. 69.

8. John S. Gottschalk, *Man and Wildlife: A Policy for Animal Damage Control* (Washington, D.C.: U.S. Department of the Interior, 1967), p. 3.

9. A. Starker Leopold (chairman), "Predator and Rodent Control in the United States. [Report of] the Special Advisory Board on Wildlife Management for the Secretary of the Interior," *Transactions 29th North American Wildlife and Natural Resources Conference* (Las Vegas, Nev., 1964), pp. 27–49; Stanley A. Cain (chairman), *Report to the Council on Environmental Quality and*

the Department of the Interior by the Advisory Committee on *Predatory Animal Control* (Ann Arbor, Mich.: Institute for Environmental Quality, 1971).

10. *Federal Register* 37, no. 27 (1972): 2875–2876.

11. Roger Caras, *Dangerous to Man* (Philadelphia: Chilton, 1964), p. 337.

12. U.S. National Park Service, *In Grizzly Country* (Washington, D.C., 1972).

13. A. McDiarmid, *Diseases of Free-Living Wild Animals*, United Nations FAO Agricultural Studies, no. 57 (Rome, 1962); James H. Steele, *Animal Disease and Human Health*, United Nations, Food and Agricultural Organization, Freedom from Hunger Campaign, Basic Study no. 3 (Rome, 1962).

14. Mary Meagher, *Brucellosis and the Yellowstone Bison*, Yellowstone National Park Information Paper no. 17 (1972).

15. McDiarmid, *Diseases of Free-Living Wild Animals*, pp. 14–15.

9. BIRD-AND-BEAST WATCHING

1. Quoted in Penelope Gilliatt, "Profile of Jean Renoir," *The New Yorker*, August 23, 1968, p. 54.

2. Black Elk, *Black Elk Speaks* . . . (Lincoln, Nebr.: University of Nebraska Press, 1961), p. 1.

3. U.S. Bureau of Sport Fisheries and Wildlife, *1970 Survey of Fishing and Hunting*, Resource Publication 95 (1972).

4. U.S. Bureau of Sport Fisheries and Wildlife, *National Wildlife Refuges, 1970*, Resource Publication 97 (1972).

5. *Scientific Activities in Fisheries and Wildlife Resources*, Science Council of Canada, Special Study no. 15, (Information Canada, 1971), p. 56.

6. John Madson and Ed Kozicky, *Game, Gunners and Biology:*

Reference Notes

The Scientific Approach to Wildlife Management (East Alton, Ill.: Winchester-Western Division of Olin Corporation, 1971), p. 22.

7. International Association of Game, Fish and Conservation Commissioners, *Proceedings, 61st Convention, 1971* (Salt Lake City, Utah, 1972), p. 205.

8. Nathaniel P. Reed, "Forecast of Things to Come—the Challenges Ahead," *ibid.*, p. 21.

9. Missouri Conservation Department, *Missouri Conservation Program: an Appraisal and Some Suggestions* (Jefferson City, Mo., 1970), p. 25.

10. Missouri Conservation Department, *Design for Conservation* (Jefferson City, Mo., 1971), p. 22.

11. John Madson and Ed Kozicky, *A Law for Wildlife: Model Legislation for a State Nongame Wildlife Conservation Program* (East Alton, Ill.: Winchester-Western Division of Olin Corporation, 1972), p. 3.

12. *Ibid.*, pp. 12, 20.

13. Richard Ruoff, legislative chairman, Washington State Sportsmen's Council, letter to the author, March 5, 1973.

14. Gilbert White, *The Natural History and Antiquities of Selborne, in the County of Southampton* (London: B. White & Son, 1789).

15. Ted Walker, "The Harpooning," *The Night Bathers / Poems* (London: Jonathan Cape, 1970), p. 25.

16. Roger Tory Peterson and James Fisher, *Wild America* (Boston: Houghton Mifflin, 1955), p. 369.

10. THE ADMINISTRATIVE STRUCTURE

1. Charles Elton, *The Ecology of Animals* (London: Methuen, 1933), 87.

2. U.S. Congress, Senate Committee on Commerce *Ocean Mam-*

mal Protection, Hearings, 92d Cong., 2d sess., serial no. 92-56 (1972), part 1, 528.

3. E. I. Dupont de Nemours Company, *Wild Game—Its Legal Status* (Wilmington, Del., 1940?).

4. "National Wildlife Federation: The Dream That Stamps Built," *National Wildlife* 10, no. 6 (1972); 26. This and many other organizations mentioned in the text are described in *Conservation Directory 1973* (Washington, D.C.: National Wildlife Federation).

5. Robert Leo Smith, review of *A Manual of Wildlife Conservation,* ed. R. D. Teague (Washington, D.C.: Wildlife Society, 1971), in *Bioscience* 21, no. 22 (1971): 1143.

6. Stewart L. Udall, "Paradise in Peril: An American Epilogue," in Prince Philip and James Fisher, *Wildlife Crisis* (New York: Cowles Co. and World Wildlife Fund, 1970), p. 209.

7. G. Carleton Ray and Kenneth S. Norris, "Managing Marine Environments," *Transactions 37th North American Wildlife and Natural Resources Conference* (1972), p. 192.

11. LEARNING ABOUT WILDLIFE

1. U.S. Federal Committee on Research Natural Areas, *A Directory of Research Natural Areas on Federal Lands of the United States* . . . (Washington, D.C.: Government Printing Office, 1968).

2. Jerry F. Franklin, Frederick C. Hall, C. T. Dyrness, and Chris Maser, *Federal Research Natural Areas in Oregon and Washington: A Guidebook for Scientists and Educators* (Portland, Ore.: U.S. Forest Service, 1972), p. 2.

3. Washington State, Natural Area Preserves Act, Chapter 119, Laws of 1972 (79.70 R. C. W.).

4. Archie Carr, *The Reptiles* (New York: Time-Life Books), 1963), pp. 172, 175.

13. DEALING WITH WILDLIFE THROUGH HABITATS

1. Joseph J. Shomon, Byron L. Ashbaugh, and Con D. Tolman, *Wildlife Habitat Improvement* (New York: National Audubon Society, 1966).

2. U.S. Agricultural Stabilization and Conservation Service, news releases, December 27, 1971, and January 14, 1972, and brochure, March 1972, on Set-Aside Program (Washington, D.C.).

3. Public Land Law Review Commission, "Fish and Wildlife Resources," *One Third of the Nation's Land: A Report to the President and to the Congress* (Washington, D.C., 1970), pp. 156–175.

4. *National Parks for the Future* (Washington, D.C.: Conservation Foundation, 1972).

5. A. Starker Leopold (chairman), "The National Wildlife Refuge System: Report of the Advisory Committee on Wildlife Management appointed by Interior Secretary Stewart L. Udall," *Transactions 33d North American Wildlife and Natural Resources Conference, 1968* (Houston, Tex., 1968), pp. 30–54.

6. U.S. Bureau of Sport Fisheries and Wildlife, *National Wildlife Refuges, 1970,* Research Publication 97 (1972), p. 5.

7. Quoted in Paul Brooks, *The House of Life* (Boston: Houghton Mifflin, 1972), p. 9.

8. Rachel Carson, *Silent Spring* (Boston: Houghton Mifflin, 1962.

14. DEALING WITH WILDLIFE DIRECTLY

1. Washington State Game Department, *Your Game Department* (Olympia, Wash., 1970), p. 1.

2. Ira N. Gabrielson, *Wildlife Conservation,* 2d ed. (New York: Macmillan, 1959), p. 193.

3. G. Bryan Harry, superintendent, Hawaii Volcanoes National Park, in letter to the author, February 8, 1973.

4. Anthony Wayne Smith, "Goats in the Parks," *National Parks and Conservation Magazine* 45, no. 11 (1971).

5. A. Starker Leopold (chairman), "Study of Wildlife Problems in National Parks. [Report of] the Special Advisory Board on Wildlife Management for the Secretary of the Interior," *Transactions 28th North American Wildlife and Natural Resources Conference, 1963* (Detroit, Mich., 1963), pp. 28–45.

6. Dan Pottier, "Quebec's Wolf-Hunting Contest Met with Distaste," *Montreal Star,* September 27, 1972, A-18.

7. Donald S. Balser, "Management of Predator Populations with Antifertility Agents," *Journal of Wildlife Management* 28, no. 2 (1964), 352–358.

8. Robert A. McCabe and Edward L. Kozicky, "A Position Paper on Predator Management," *Journal of Wildlife Management* 36, no. 2 (1972), 394.

15. DEALING WITH PEOPLE

1. Wildlife Society, Bylaws . . . Approved on April 19, 1971, p. 3.

2. Edmund R. Belak, Jr., "The Outdoor Magazine Revisited," *Journal of Environmental Education* 4, no. 1 (1972), 15–19.

3. National Wildlife Federation, "Environmental Quality Index" [title varies], *National Wildlife* 7, no. 5 (1969), 2–13; 8, no. 6 (1970), 25–40; 9, no. 6 (1971), 25–40; 11, no. 3 (1973), 25–32.

4. John Madson and Ed Kozicky, *Principles of Game Management* (1962) and *Game, Gunners and Biology* (1971).

5. George Shaftel, *Conserving Our Wildlife: An Introductory Guide for the Teaching of Conservation Problems Relating to*

Reference Notes

Wildlife (San Francisco: Standard Oil Co. of California, 1962), p. 12.

6. League of Conservation Voters, *How Your Congressman Voted on Critical Environmental Issues* [in 1971], (Washington, D.C., 1972), 1 p. folding chart. The League publishes a similar chart for senatorial votes.

7. David L. Erickson and G. Norman van Tubergen, "The Wolf Men, *"Journal of Environmental Education 4, no. 1 (1971),* 26–30.

8. Public Land Law Review Commission, "Fish and Wildlife Resources," *One Third of the Nation's Land* . . . (Washington, D.C., 1970), pp 156–175; Lloyd W. Swift, "Review of the Report on Fish and Wildlife Resources on Public Lands," in *What's Ahead for Our Public Lands?* ed. Hamilton K. Pyles (Washington, D.C.: Natural Resources Council of America, 1970).

9. Emily Stewart Leavitt and others, *Animals and their Legal Rights* (Washington, D. C.: Animal Welfare Institute, 1970).

10. *Position Statements of the Wildlife Society on Environmental Issues* . . . (Washington, D.C.: Wildlife Society 1972), p. 9.

11. C. R. Mitchell, Chief General Claims Examiner, Province of Saskatchewan, letters to the author, February 14 and March 22, 1973.

12. Odom Fanning, "Be a Government Conservationist and Help Preserve Our Heritage of Natural Resources," *Catalyst* 2, no. 3 (1972), 28–30.

13. Fred G. Evenden, "The 1971 Graduate Placement Study," *Wildlife Society News* 138 (1972), 3.

16. THE SOURCE OF THE ETHIC

1. *Position Statements of the Wildlife Society on Environmental Issues* . . . (Washington, D.C.: Wildlife Society 1972), p. 16.

2. René Dubos, *A God Within* (New York: Charles Scribner's Sons, 1972), pp. 153–174.

17. THE ETHIC IN MOTION

1. Archibald MacLeish, *A Continuing Journey* (Boston: Houghton Mifflin, 1967), p. 41.

2. *Position Statements of the Wildlife Society on Environmental Issues* . . . (Washington, D.C.: Wildlife Society 1972), p. 13.

3. Alan S. Krug, "Firearm Ownership and Crime Rates," *Colorado Outdoors* 20, no. 4 (1971):1–4.

4. John S. Gottschalk, *Man and Wildlife: A Policy for Animal Damage Control* (Washington, D.C: U.S. Department of the Interior, 1967), pp. 1–2.

5. Marylin Bender, "The Gun Business on the Defensive," *New York Times,* March 4, 1973, sec. 3:1.

6. Stuart Hampshire, *Morality and Pessimism* (Cambridge: For the University Press, 1972), pp. 4, 36, 37.

❧ *For Further Reading*

Allen, Durward L. *Our Wildlife Legacy*. Rev. ed. New York: Funk and Wagnalls, 1962.

Burger, George V. *Practical Wildlife Management*. New York: Winchester Press, 1973.

Carrington, Richard, and the editors of *Life*. *The Mammals*. New York: Time-Life Books, 1963.

Carson, Gerald. *Men, Beasts, and Gods*. New York: Charles Scribner's Sons, 1972.

Dasmann, Raymond F. *Environmental Conservation*. 2d ed. New York: Wiley, 1968.

———. *Wildlife Biology*. New York: Wiley, 1964.

Ehrenfeld, David W. *Conserving Life on Earth*. New York: Oxford University Press, 1972.

Guggisberg, C. A. W. *Man and Wildlife*. New York: Arco, 1970.

Hutchings, Monica M., and Caver, Mavis. *Man's Dominion: Our Violation of the Animal World*. London: Rupert Hart-Davis, 1970.

Laycock, George. *The Alien Animals: The Story of Imported Wildlife*. New York: Ballantine, 1970.

Leopold, Aldo. *Game Management*. New York: Charles Scribner's Sons, 1933.

   A classic in the history of the American wildlife conservation movement.

Lindsey, Alton A., Schmelz, Damian V., and Nichols, Stanley A. *Natural Areas in Indiana and Their Preservation* (Notre Dame, Ind.: American Midland Naturalist, Notre Dame University, 1970).

McNulty, Faith. *Must They Die? The Strange Case of the Prairie Dog and the Black-footed Ferret*. New York: Audubon/Ballantine, 1972.

Nash, Roderick, ed. *The American Environment: Readings in the History of Conservation*. Reading, Mass.: Addison-Wesley, 1968.

Contains a bibliography on the history of the wildlife conservation movement.

National Research Council, National Academy of Sciences, *Land Use and Wildlife Resources*. Washington, D.C.: 1970.

Ortega y Gasset, José. *Meditations on Hunting*. New York: Charles Scribner's Sons, 1972.

Peterson, Roger Tory, and the editors of *Life*. *The Birds*. New York: Time-Life Books, 1963.

Potter, Dale R., Sharpe, Kathryn M., and Hendee, John C. *Human Behavior Aspects of Fish and Wildlife Conservation: An Annotated Bibliography*, U.S. Forest Service General Technical Report PNW-4. Portland, Ore., 1973.

Contains 995 entries, with "keyword" index and author index.

Shepard, Paul. *The Tender Carnivore and the Sacred Game*. New York: Charles Scribner's Sons, 1973.

Implications of man's primate heritage and hunting forebears.

Strong, Douglas H. *The Conservationists*. Menlo Park, Calif.: Addison-Wesley, 1971.

Discusses Henry David Thoreau, Frederick Law Olmsted, George Perkins Marsh, Gifford Pinchot, John Muir, Kirtley Mather, Aldo Leopold, Theodore Roosevelt, and Stewart Udall.

U.S. Congress, House Committee on Merchant Marine and Fisheries. *A Compilation of Federal Laws Relating to Conservation and Development of Our Nation's Fish and Wildlife Resources, Environmental Quality, and Oceanography*. Committee Print, 1972.

Vosburgh, John, *Living with Your Land*. New York: Charles Scribner's Sons, 1969.

Wildlife Society. *A Manual of Wildlife Conservation*. Washington, D.C., 1971.

——. *Wildlife Management Techniques*, 3d ed. Washington, D.C., 1971.

Yee, J. E. *The Concern for Conservation in the United States: A Selected Bibliography*. U.S. Department Interior Library, Bibliography series no. 13. 1969.

❧ Index

WHERE an animal, such as bear, is the subject of special discussion in the text, it is indexed separately. Where it is only mentioned in passing, it is indexed under a category: exotic species, furbearers, game species, non-game species, marine mammals, predators and raptors, rodents, sea birds, or waterfowl.

Index

Index

Index

⚹ *About the Author*

Victor B. Scheffer is a charter member of the Wildlife Society (founded 1937)—a North American organization of professional biologists and administrators in wildlife conservation. He served for more than thirty years as a biologist in the Forest Service, National Park Service, Fish and Wildlife Service, and National Marine Fisheries Service. He was sent to Antarctica in 1964 on the State Department's first team of Antarctic Observers. For his studies of marine mammals, he received in 1965 the Department of the Interior's Distinguished Service Award. He retired in 1969 to write and to lecture in vertebrate zoology at the University of Washington. His book *The Year of the Whale* was awarded the John Burroughs Medal in 1970 for the best book in the field of natural history. He is also the author of *The Year of the Seal* and *The Seeing Eye*.